Eat Goulash and Enjoy Beer in Prague Like a Local

Roman Jelinek

Copyright © 2016 Roman Jelinek

The moral right of the author has been asserted

Apart from any fair dealing for the purposes of research or private study or criticism or review, as permitted under the Copyright, Designs and Patents Act 1988, this publication may only be reproduced, stored or transmitted, in any form or by any means, with the prior permission in writing of the author, or in the case of reprographic reproduction in accordance with the terms of licences issued by the Copyright Licensing Agency.

Published by www.pragueczechtravel.com

Please direct any comments or suggestions about this document to:
roman@pragueczechtravel.com

To Alena.
For always being happy with me, even at 6 in the morning.

And to Dorian.
For waking us up at 6 in the morning.

Contents

Introduction 1

What Do You Feel Like Eating 9

What Kind of Restaurant Experience Do You Want? 23

How to Get to the Restaurant 55

You Are at the Restaurant 71

Conversation Topics While You Eat 93

Hope to See You Around 113

This Will Help You Blend 115

Introduction

It has probably happened to you before. You walk out of your hotel room, take a wrong turn, and get lost. Suddenly the streets are almost empty except for the locals going about their daily business. You aren't in a hurry, so you walk into a restaurant and find that for the first time on your trip, you are the only tourist. With smiles and nods, you and the waiter understand each other, even though you're not sure what you ordered. You gaze around the restaurant and see a family at the table next to you chatting among themselves and a lone man sitting with a cigarette and a beer. Your meal arrives and it's like nothing you have eaten before.

You were lost, you had no idea what you were eating, and you understood nothing that was said. It was the best part of your vacation.

I wrote this book to enable you to enjoy the local experience in Prague. I will not be dictating specifically where you should go or what you need to see. Instead, I will make you comfortable with Prague and its people. Knowing the intricacies of a city and its culture provides you with the ability to leave the tourist group behind and walk into a restaurant that's been serving delicious goulash and beer to locals for generations.

How often do you eat out at the tourist spots in your hometown? My guess is never—tourist spots are crowded, loud, and expensive, and the food is overcooked or still frozen.

Prague is a city flooded with tourists, especially in the summer. Charles Bridge is 10 meters wide and over 500 meters long, yet during the summer, the tips of your toes are always pressing against someone else's heels. Tourists need to eat and drink. Restaurants lie waiting, eager to fill the tourists' tummies—and lighten their wallets.

Prague is a 'tourist trap' city. The major tourist sites (Charles Bridge, Prague Castle, Old Town Square) have restaurants specifically designed for tourists. The restaurant owners know their patrons have few options because most visitors will not venture far from established tourist zones. Tourists worry because they don't speak the language, and they also worry they will get lost, mugged, and left for dead. Restaurant owners take advantage of these frightened tourists. They raise the prices and lower the quality of the food they serve.

Hopefully you are reading this book because you are not afraid to venture beyond the established tourist zone. You want to experience the real Prague—the Prague locals know.

You do not need to be especially brave to experience the real Prague. You do not need to walk down unlit alleys for delicious food and cheap beer. Good local restaurants are usually just a block away from the tourist ones. As we've already discussed, locals never eat at tourist restaurants. Why would they? So why should you?

This book will teach you everything you need to know to have a pleasant and trouble-free local experience. Don't worry—Czechs are good-hearted and will tolerate your struggle to speak their tongue-twisting language with a smile. You do not need to understand Czech to enjoy a local restaurant. With the advice in this book, you will be able to find a restaurant, order a goulash, and drink liters of world-famous Czech beer. You will eat authentic Czech meals prepared for locals.

In addition to having an authentic experience, you'll save money too. How much, you ask? A large half pint of Pilsner Urquell in the made-for-tourist restaurants costs 100 CZK ($5.50 USD). A block away at a local restaurant an identical beer costs 26 CZK ($1.40 USD). A meal of meat and dumplings is around 80 CZK ($4.40 USD) in the local restaurant; expect to pay almost double that in a made-for-tourists restaurant.

In this book I cover everything I can think of to turn you into a Prague local. If I missed anything, let me know. Write me an e-mail, and I'll try to help you experience the real Prague.

Better to be Underprepared

The prepared traveler visits their local library and spends the afternoon reading all they can get their hands on about their destination. They study maps, badger friends who have been there, and send e-mails to the embassy. They end up knowing more about their destination than the locals. They know the history, the culture, when the barbarians invaded, and the name of the president's current mistress. It's an obsession—they need to know everything before they step on the airplane.

Introduction

They don't stop with simply doing research. They go to their bank and exchange currency, they go to the doctor and ask for shots, and they study the ingredients of the food served and bring the perfect ratio of antacid to indigestion pills.

Because you are reading this book, you belong somewhere in the prepared traveler category. You are researching Prague because you want to be ready. Nothing wrong with that. But hopefully you have a little 'surprise me' traveler in you as well because that is the attitude you need to venture off into the local restaurants.

Sometimes the 'surprise me' traveler does not even know what country they are in. They choose a destination with the spin of the globe, they pack a passport, a pair of socks, underwear, a toothbrush, jeans, a T-shirt, and a sweater, and off they go. Depending on the temperature when they arrive, they will either put on a sweater or take off a shirt.

They do absolutely no research about their destination because they want it to be a surprise. They come out of the airport wide-eyed and confused. The first question they ask is, "Do you accept dollars?" The second question is to the taxi driver: "What do people do around here for fun?"

To experience Prague like a local, you will need be less prepared and more open to surprises. Nothing can prepare you for what you might find walking into a restaurant with no English on the door.

Regardless of whether you are the 'surprise me' traveler or the all-prepared traveler, here are a few things you should know:

- In the winter (November to February) you need a winter jacket. In the summer you need shorts.
- You can buy toothpaste here.
- Beer in tourist spots costs 50 CZK ($2.78 USD). In non-tourist spots it cost 23 CZK ($1.27 USD).
- You do not need to learn the Czech language to order a 'svickova na smetane'. Most places in Prague have an English menu that will say 'slices of pork with sliced bread dumplings'.
- Charles Bridge was first built in 1360.
- Prague is on the metric system.
- Electricity in the Czech Republic is 220V and AC 50Hz.
- Tip at a restaurant between 10 and 15 percent.
- Use your thumb for counting. One = thumb. Two = thumb and index finger.

- For couples, a man should enter the restaurant first (to ensure that it is safe and to take the first punch if necessary).
- Dates appear as day/month/year, so my birthday is 25/04/19#6
- You will get slippers if you visit someone's home.
- Wear jeans to the opera at your own risk of being frowned upon.
- Commas are decimal points and decimals commas. Two and a half is 2,50; two thousand is 2.000
- A waiter will not take your plate unless your fork and knife are together.
- Restaurants are for socialising so tables are not always private. If the place is full and there are two open places at your table don't be surprised if somebody joins you.
- There were 62 people murdered last year. A million were not. Prague is safe.

What Do You Feel Like Eating

So you walked around Prague all morning and you are ready to fill that empty stomach. Fortunately, you never have to go far to find food. Czech people enjoy eating out. During Communism there was only one channel on TV, so food, friends, and beer became the best entertainment.

Hopefully you did a lot of walking because Czech cuisine contains plenty of calories. Unless you cashed in your flight home and are planning to jog back, expect to gain a few pounds.

There are many dishes to choose from, but they can be simplified into two main types: it's going to be a sauce with meat and dumplings, or it's going to be breaded and fried.

The Meat – Sauce - Dumpling Combo

The most popular meat, sauce, and dumpling combination is goulash. Goulash offers a thick and spicy sauce with chunks of tender, stewed beef and dumplings. Dumplings are a kind of white bread that is really efficient at absorbing sauce. Standard procedure is to place the meat in your mouth, slice off a piece of dumpling, and slide it around the plate on your fork to soak up the sauce. As soon as you swallow the meat, insert the sauce-soaked dumpling into your mouth to create the perfect aftertaste. Only practice can determine how much to soak the dumpling so that your last piece of dumpling soaks up all the remaining sauce. After a few plates, you should be able to end with a perfectly clean plate.

With the basic arrangement of meat, sauce, and dumpling, you will find many varieties. For example, the meat can be beef (in many different forms), or it can be duck, turkey, rabbit, or wild boar. Each type of meat has its own sauce to complement it. For example, beef in a more tender form is combined with a white creamy sauce called 'svickova', while wild boar is served with a side of red cabbage sauce.

When you look at a Czech lunch menu, most of the items will be an assortment of meat, sauce, and dumpling combinations. This food is in a section of the menu called 'Hotovki' (finished food) because it is precooked and ready to serve. You will receive your food in minutes because the kitchen has pots that are boiling and filled with all the different sauces and meats. All the cook has to do is grab a plate, place five dumplings in a crescent moon around the edge of the plate, scoop his spatula into the bubbling pot, and pour it over the dumplings. It's fast, it's cheap, and best of all, it's good.

I do not know how to describe what the food tastes like. Be adventurous and pick a random combination every time to taste the different varieties. Look for the word 'knedlik' (dumpling) to find the section on the menu with the meat, sauce, and dumpling combos. For starters, you cannot go wrong with either goulash or svickova.

What is goulash anyway?

Up until the 19th century, Hungary was cowboy country. Nobody called them cowboys, but they performed the same function as modern cowboys with pickup trucks—they moved cows from point A to point B.

Hungary has a Great Plains called Puszta, which was home to herds of cattle consisting of more than 10,000 heads. The Hungarian cowboys (without pickup trucks) would drive the herds through most of central Europe to sell them in the markets of major communities like Venice, Nuremberg, and Moravia.

Unlike cowboys in the West with their campfire pans of sizzling bacon and eggs, Hungarian cowboys feasted on goulash cooked in a large black cauldron.

How do you make goulash? First of all, let's get this out of the way—goulash is not health food. The main ingredient is meat, but it is closely followed by lard, flour, and salt—great ingredients if you need to build energy for a full day of cattle herding through Europe, not so great if you sit at a desk all day.

Now that we understand that element of goulash, take quality, well-exercised meat from the shoulder, cut it up into bite-sized cubes, and toss it into a large pot. Add calorie-dripping lard for flavor and sizzle. Chop up a few onions and throw them in. Add water, beef broth, garlic, and finally paprika for spice. Put the pot on the stove and let the ingredients congeal. Add flour for desired thickness.

A few hours later, the delicious smell of lard-filled beef shoulder and onion will penetrate your house. Depending on the quantity of calories required, eat the goulash as a thick soup, or—as most Czechs prefer to get that extra shot of calories—fill the side of the plate with a beach of sauce-absorbing dumplings.

I have no idea how the Hungarian cowboys were able to eat goulash and work because after a plate of goulash, I always need a three-hour nap.

Breaded and Deep Fried

How many foods can be dusted with flour, soaked in egg yolk, rolled in a pile of dried breadcrumbs, and deep fried? You're probably already familiar with the German schnitzel that uses this process on pork steak, but the famous Czech ingenuity has taken this concept and tried it with almost everything that is solid.

Buns don't last more than a day. If you buy four fresh buns in the morning, by evening they are mushy and inedible. A week later they are hard as a rock. What to do? Take the rock bun and grate it to form the little breadcrumbs. Maybe Czechs overestimate the number of buns they will eat during the day because there are always plenty of hard buns ready to be converted into breadcrumbs.

You will find the following breaded and fried foods in most local restaurants: pork, veal, chicken, Hermelín cheese, Edam cheese, cauliflower, and mushrooms.

The 'smažený' (covered in breadcrumbs and deep-fried) meats like pork, chicken, and veal are usually served with 'bramborovej salad' (potato salad), 'važený brambor' (cooked potatoes), or 'hranolky' (fries).

Most Czech meals contain meat, so what do you do if you need to give your stomach a day off and offer it an easy-to-process, non-meat meal? It's not so easy to do. There are non-meat options, but they're not lighter on the stomach juices. To hide the fact that there is no meat, the non-meat meals are 'smažený'. They are hidden behind a coat of breadcrumbs and fried until they're meat-color brown. To complete the illusion, they take up the exact spot on the plate usually reserved for the meat. Don't want meat? Have a light and healthy cauliflower dipped in breadcrumbs and deep fried with your potato.

Need dairy? Try the breaded and deep-fried cheese. Breaded mushrooms are popular for those looking to eat something from the forest that wasn't hunted.

All the above non-meats are served with cooked potatoes and a hearty, creamy tartar sauce. A beer is mandatory to offset the taste of the grease.

Another traditional non-meat meal is potato pancakes. In this dish, potatoes are grated and mixed with egg and flour. The resulting mush is poured

What Do You Feel Like Eating

pancake-style into a deep pool of oil. It is unhealthy, feels like a brick in the stomach, and is ridiculously delicious.

There is no getting around it—while in Czech, your stomach will not get any rest.

A Pig's Last Day and His Delicious Knee

Once a year family and friends from a village gather together and celebrate. Knives are sharpened, troughs are cleaned and large charcoal black pots are placed around the butcher table. Everybody has a part to perform. The men and older boys chop, slice, scoop, and ground. The girls walk around with rags and mops maintaining a clean work area. Wives and mothers make sure the men are well fed throughout the day while they hack and sweat. The youngest and most energetic boy has the honour to start the festivities - catch and hold the frightened pig as it senses his final hour has arrived. With cheer and clapping as encouragement the boy chases, corners and finally holds the pig down. The day officially begins. The day is called zabijačka - pig slaughter day. What started in the early morning as a frightened pig ends by afternoon as sausages, hams, lard, bacon and pork bellies.

Nothing is spared, everything is eaten in one form or another. Even the blood does not go to waste. The blood is drained into a deep pot and heated, then with a small wooden paddle the blood soup is stirred for hours to prevent coagulation. The smell of blood soup fills the air as friends huddle around and inhale deeply. A line of the hungry forms with bowls and spoon in hand.

The intestines are used to create sausage wraps which are filled with ground pig meat soaked in its own blood. As the sausage is cooked the air expands and pushes from the inside against the intestine skin. When the fork punctures the tight intestine skin a gratifying explosion of blood and meat splurges across the plate.

The tongue and skin is chewed at and nibbled throughout the day. All the remaining pig pieces, including bone, are mixed together with head cheese and pig skin broth to form a pig jelly desert called tlačenka. By the end of the afternoon, the only thing left are the big bones. Each young girls take a bone and throw it across the yard- the first bone scooped up by a dog signals which girl will be the first to marry.

In essence a pig is a big ball of meat held up by four rickety stick legs. Which is why it is surprising that for Czech's the most delicious meat of the pig is in the knee.

Order a pig knee and you will be presented with a cavemanish hunk of bone on a wooden cutting board. After the obligatory claims that you will never be able to eat it all you will start to doubt yourself as you peel away at the juicy meat that just slips off the bone. The abundant dose of fat and crispy skin will quickly turn you into a knee praiser and the next time you see a pig your eyes will dart straight to the legs. Served with brown bread, horse radish and mustard you will peal meat with one hand, chew on bread with the other and use both to washing it down with beer - like a true caveman.

The Miserable Cow and Eating him Raw

Czech cows have miserable lives. They do not spend their lives roaming open plains in the sunshine. They spend their days in a dank barn with the limited exercise of move head down to eat and up to look around. This is unfortunate not only for them but also for those eating them. Cows lacking exercise can not produce lean and tender steaks. There are plenty of beef options on the menu but you will notice when the plate comes that the meat is well hidden in a sauce or served raw.

To be frightened of raw meat is prudent. Always wash hands thoroughly after handling, vigorously wipe the cutting board with hot water and make certain the meat does not touch anything in the fridge. Salmonella poisoning is why every home chef cooks the meat just a little bit longer, just to be sure. That is why for most people tatarak is considered a brave food. It is a mound of raw minced beef. Exactly the same as you buy at the butcher and which you are not suppose to touch with your hands.

To prepare the chef, using his hands, moulds the meat into a volcano and plops it in the middle of the plate. Into the crater he breaks a raw egg. Around the volcano he creates little piles of condiments: diced onion (uncooked of course), various spices, salts, ketchup, mustards. Ion a separate plate are a stack of deep fried bread slices. Design wise it looks pretty but now you have to eat it.

Take two forks and start to mix and mash everything together until you have an evenly distributed blob of meat. Next take a slice of deep fried bread and spread the garlic over it, both sides if you like garlic. Now scoop the meat and spread a thick layer on the bread. The final and most difficult step is to forget everything you have ever heard about raw meat and swallow.

Show the miserable cow some respect and eat him raw, but I would strongly suggest that you avoid the tatarak if it is being offered at a discount.

Reading the Menu

Menus are broken up into the following general sections:

• **'k pivu' (with Beer).** These are usually small portions of food that are ideal with a beer. Consider them something to munch on while you drink your beer, but they are not appetizers—they are small meals. Eat them when you are not hungry enough to eat a full meal but want to avoid drinking on an empty stomach. You will find goodies like potato pancakes, pickled sausage with onion, raw meat with egg and ketchup, and some kind of see-through Jell-O filled with meat that I am still unable to completely identify.

• **Polevky (Soups).** Here you will find two or three soups to choose from. Czech cuisine has many different types of soups, some of which will sound familiar, like goulash soup and potato soup. Then there are others that are not that common, like a red soup made from cow stomach and a black soup made by boiling pig's blood. I was hesitant at first, especially with the blood soup, but they are all tasty and the locals eat them, so you can be sure they won't kill you.

• **Hotovi (Done Food).** Here you will find all the precooked and ready-to-serve food. This is where most of the meat, sauce, and dumpling combinations are. This section is served fast and is usually very inexpensive because it is served in bulk. Some people even bring their own pots to be filled, which they take home to heat up on the stove.

• **Hlavni Jedlo (Main Food).** This section contains food requiring preparation as well as specialties of the restaurant. For example, if the restaurant offers Mexican tortillas, you will find them in this section.

• **Přílohy (Side Dishes).** Here you will find a list of side dishes to choose from. Typically, you will find potatoes (boiled, mashed, roasted), fries, American fries (potato wedges), rice, and dumplings. You can order what you want, but be careful with dumplings—the waiter will give you a queer look if you order dumplings with a non-sauce meal. For example, it would be odd if you ordered a 'řízek' (schnitzel) with a side of dumplings because you would be eating the dumplings dry, and that's just not done.

• **Omáčky a dressingy (Sauces and Dressings).** Here you will find ketchup, mustard, tartar sauce, and salad dressing. There will not be a bottle of ketchup and mustard on the table. If you want them with your fries, you need to order them. They are served in a little side dish. Don't forget that for foods requiring tartar sauce—breaded cheese, mushrooms, cauliflower—you will need to order the tartar sauce separately. Oddly, even though everybody has tartar sauce with these meals, you need to request it.

• **Dezert (Dessert).** Czech desserts are sweet but not ridiculously sweet like some Western favorites. Czechs are fond of their desserts though. There are little shops all over Prague called 'cukrárny' (sweet shops) that sell nothing but desserts—enter at your own risk.

What Kind of Restaurant Experience

Do You Want?

Prague has a reputation for poor service at restaurants. Sometimes it is well deserved, but in most cases I have found the service satisfactory—although I must admit to being more tolerant than most.

A distinction needs to be made. In Prague there are two types of restaurants: the restaurants in the tourist district that cater to tourists and the restaurants catering to locals.

The few times that I went to a tourist restaurant the service was good. It was the kind and prompt service you would expect from any Western restaurant. That is because tourists, especially Western tourists, are used to tipping based on service. The waiter gets paid based on a service level—the better the service, the higher the tip.

This is not always the case for restaurants that cater to locals—especially in small towns. The service level is a couple notches lower because locals do not tip as gratuitously as Westerners.

During Communism, no one tipped, so the mentality of waiters was different. A waiter would be paid regardless of the customer's satisfaction level and regardless of how well the restaurant was doing. A paycheck was guaranteed to arrive every month regardless of his behavior towards the customers. There was no motivation for the waiter to please. It was actually quite the opposite—the waiter hoped the customers never came back. The less busy the restaurant, the less work for him, and he got paid regardless. To make matters worse, the waiter would purposely delay collecting the bill. He wanted the current customers to stay as long as possible because if they left, he would have to serve a whole new group of hungry people. That's work.

Fortunately, Communism is gone, but the shadows remain. Remnants of the communist waiter remain. Sometimes you get a sense the waiter feels he is doing you a favor by serving you. He could be resting, but no, he will get up and go to the kitchen for your food.

But a waiter rolling his eyes will not bother you. You are visiting local restaurants because you want the local experience. And if the waiter is sitting at a table smoking and laughing with the chef while you are starving, you can proudly say that you are living like the locals.

Beer Signs Tell You Where and What

To find an authentic Czech restaurant, turn onto a side street and walk for 10 minutes— away from tourists. Restaurants are easy to spot—not by a sign indicating the name of the restaurant, but by a large glowing sign stating the beer they serve.

Each restaurant serves one brand of beer because each restaurant is sponsored by a beer company. The beer company supplies them with tablecloths, coasters, glasses, and a large glowing sign to display outside the restaurant.

The signs are big and they glow. Simply walk down a street and look for the beer signs. They stick out into the street just above the door. By looking down side streets, you can immediately determine whether there are restaurants in that direction.

Beer companies choose the restaurants in which they want their beer served. So the type of beer served provides you with an indication of the kind of restaurant it is.

Pilsner Urquell, Gambrinus – A Place to Eat a Good Meal with Quality Service and Ambiance

Looking for a nice place to sit with friends and eat good local food? Pilsner Urquell has a brand to protect. They need to be seen as the original and highest quality beer in the Czech Republic, so they do not allow just anybody to serve their beer. Only restaurants that meet their standards of quality, service, and overall dining experience are allowed to represent the beer.

The standards of Pilsner Urquell restaurants resemble those of the better Irish pubs in the West. Usually there is a smoking section and a nonsmoking section, the bathrooms are clean, the food is fresh, and the beer pipes are clean (a certificate hangs on the bar wall that proves it).

Pilsner Urquell restaurants are where I take visitors on their first day in Prague. They provide the least dramatic transition from what Westerners are accustomed to.

Krušovice, Kozel, Radegast, Budvar – A Place to Drink Beer, Smoke, and Chat with 'Professional' Drinkers

Krušovice, Kozel, Radegast, and Budvar are risky because they have lower standards for the kinds of places that are allowed to sell their beers. Actually, as far as I can tell, they have no standards.

If you decide to enter a restaurant with these beer signs above the door, then do not be surprised at what you find.

You might find that:

- The place is as smoky as London is foggy.

- There is a guy sitting in a corner with half a beer in front of him. He looks like he has not moved from that spot in two weeks.

- The tablecloths are washed once a year and therefore contain historic samples of the menu.

- The bathrooms are washed when the tablecloths are washed.

- There will be slot machines. A guy with a cigarette dangling from his mouth and a beer in his hand will be playing when you arrive and when you leave. If you come back a few days later, he will still be playing.

- Everybody knows everybody. You would be right to suspect that they drink beer together every day.
- The cook comes out of the kitchen every 20 minutes and has a cigarette break at the bar.

In other words, some of these restaurants are a shade darker. But don't worry—you will not be shot and tossed in the Dumpster. It is just that these restaurants cater to the local clientele who really enjoy beer and are not particularly concerned with ambiance or when the tablecloth was washed. These restaurants are like those you find in small, rural towns—they are where the beer-drinking locals hang out.

Of course, not all Krušovice and Kozel are shady, but some of them are. I am just warning you so that you are not surprised when you enter one and get scared into running to the nearest tourist restaurant.

Even with these drawbacks, there is a reason to try these restaurants: the food is inexpensive. A complete meal of five dumplings, meat, sauce, and a pint of beer will cost less than 100 CZK ($5 USD). And nine times out of 10, the food will be delicious. The best meals I've had were always in these shady places. The chef is amongst friends, and he has been making their meals for years.

I strongly suggest that you visit these hardcore local restaurants at least once. It provides an authentic Prague experience—smoking cough included. Don't worry—nobody is going to hurt you. They are too focused on drinking beer and complaining about the government. And if a few red-faced men suddenly stand up, click beer mugs, and start singing, don't be afraid to join in. They will be glad to have a new member in their daily beer-drinking club.

Tourist Places to Avoid Eating and Drinking

You are on vacation, you are visiting Prague, so you should see all you can see. But when it comes to eating and drinking, try to stay away from the tourist spots. They are tourist traps. They know you are ignorant, so they jack up the prices and hope you don't notice. Most people are too timid to veer off the guided path without English signs on the door, so it works. Tourists in tourist spots are trapped

Eating in a restaurant for tourists is like buying popcorn at the movie theater. They have you trapped, they know you have no other option, so they take advantage of you. It is not just in Prague—it is everywhere.

Fortunately, in Prague you are not forced to eat in the tourist spots. It is not dangerous to drift off into some side street and look for eats. Locals enjoy eating out, so there are plenty of restaurants to choose from. In Prague you cannot walk two minutes without finding a local restaurant. The beer is cheaper, the food is cheaper and better, and best of all, there are no tourists—just the peaceful hum of the Czech language and people going about their normal day.

Here are a couple maps of the center of Prague—east of the river and west of the river. I have highlighted the five main tourist spots. Go visit these places because that's where the historic and interesting sites of Prague are, but don't eat there unless you want to pay a little extra and listen to a family shout at each other in Italian. When you are hungry, walk one block out from these highlighted zones into a whole other world.

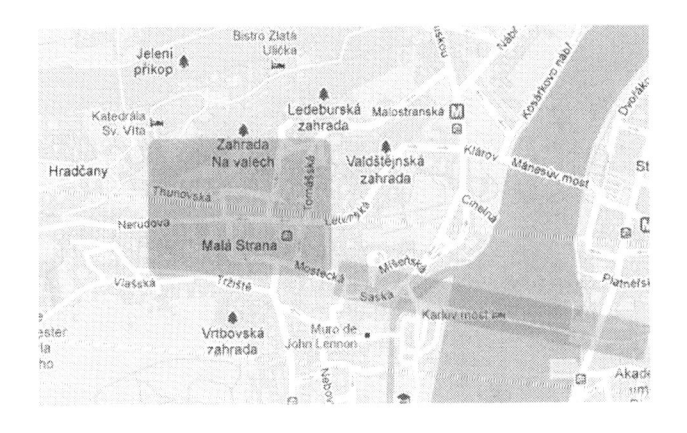

Here you see the west side of the river. Tourists cross the Charles Bridge (highlighted) and then walk up to the Prague Castle on the top of the hill. The entire area walking up to the castle and around the castle (highlighted) is a tourist hot spot. During the summer season you will be shoulder to shoulder with almost every nationality in the world except Czech.

Here is the east side of the river. Again, tourists cross the Charles Bridge (highlighted) and walk toward the Old Town Square (highlighted). The entire walk from the Charles Bridge to the Old Town Square is a tourist hot spot. I remember once I was walking along this crowed street and, without checking the price, bought an ice cream from an innocent little stand. It was nothing special, just a normal cone with one scoop of ice cream. It cost me 100 CZK ($5 USD).

On the bottom right of the map is Wenceslas Square (highlighted). It is the street where the Czech people gather for revolutions. The last one was in 1989 when the people revolted against Communism and peacefully demanded the Communists leave the government. Today it is a tourist hot spot. The square contains the very large national museum, the statue of Wenceslas on his horse, and a lot of McDonald's restaurants. Tourists love this square. Go see it, but I can assure you that is not where the locals go (until the next revolution).

Hopefully I have comforted you enough to enable you to walk off the tram and find a local restaurant.

Local Experience: Turnstile, sit-down, no waiters

Normally, a restaurant in which you enter through a turnstile should be avoided. But in Prague there is an exception - Havelská Koruna. It has other quirks: It is in the tourist zone, but meals are offered in their Czech names. The staff do not and have no inclination to speak English. There are no waiters. And most importantly, unlike most food places with a turnstile, this restaurant makes great food. It is where the locals go if they are stuck in the tourist zone.

You walk in and with no explanation receive a piece of paper. You grab a tray and wait in line. Almost every classic Czech meal can be had here. All the food is laid out in trays, buffet style. If you know what you want and what it looks like, you will have no trouble at all. Just point to it, and a smile-less staffer will reach out for your plate and say 'Kolik knedliko?' (You chose a meat sauce, and dumplings go with meat sauce. She is asking, 'How many dumplings?') Use your fingers, and with a smile-less nod, that exact number of 'knedliky' will be arranged in a crescent along the edge of your plate.

A digression. As I mentioned earlier, most Czech meals are a meat sauce with side of dumplings. I still do not know all the meat sauces by their names. For simplicity, I keep them mentally organized by their colors. There is a brown sauce, a white sauce, an orange sauce, and a red sauce. My favorite is the white one, but they are all delicious. You cannot lose by randomly cycling through all the colors. If you have tried all the meat-sauce foods and want to try a dry food, you open up a whole new opportunity for side dishes. For non-sauce foods (dry food) you have fries, potatoes, potato salad, rice, American fries (British fries to Americans) — in other words, everything besides dumplings. As I mentioned earlier, if you order a dry food and ask for dumplings as a side, expect to see the staff circling fingers around their ears.

With your plate of sauce and dumplings on your tray, keep moving down the line. Next you will see an older man standing behind a beer tap with one hand on the top of the tap and another hand reaching for a mug. He is waiting for you to choose between large or small. The question of whether you want a beer is not discussed. You want a beer. Do you want a large or a small? If you do not want a beer, point to the small. A small smile for you, and then he looks intently at the beer flowing down the inside of the mug, causing a growing head of foam. He pushes the tap back up precisely when the foam is five millimeters above the lip of the glass. As he places the mug on your tray, the impact forces the head to break, and a stream of foam cascades down the outside of the glass and onto your tray. This is normal.

Another digression. You have about 30 seconds to witness a miracle. Pick up the mug and notice that near the top is a short black horizontal line. Look at the line and notice the liquid beer is far below the line. Your natural instinct is to cry foul, believing that once again the ignorant tourist is being taken advantage of. But in this case it is not so. Watch the line and the dance unfolding between the liquid and the foam. Before your eyes, as the foam returns to its natural liquid state, the beer will rise up to the line. The beer rises and the foam lowers. Michelangelo can sculpt a human figure out of a stone. A Czech barman can make the beer rise and stop exactly at the short black line.

With a beer, food on your plate, and a piece of paper with squiggles marked by the sauce lady and beer man, find a table and enjoy.

The seating is another pleasant surprise from this turnstile restaurant. You can choose to sit in a sunlit airy section or in a more secluded section with wide and long booths. If you need another beer, take your piece of paper and ask the old man for another. He will mark another squiggle and perform his miracle.

When you are full of sauces and beer, drowsiness will quickly set in. It is time to go. Put your tray away, take your piece of paper, and head for the cashier. No words required, just give her the paper and she will decode the squiggles into buttons to press on the register. A numbers pops up, you pay, and out you go.

Local Experience: Standing Deli

It is said that the best things in life are the simple ones. The Czech deli is an example of this truism. The complexities of a restaurant—finding a table, ordering drinks, reading through the menu, waiting for the waiter, ordering, waiting, getting the bill, tipping—are all avoided at a Czech deli.

Czech delis provide enough variety for a complete meal and a place to stand to enjoy it. It is a restaurant at its most simplest.

There are two components to a deli meal: the meat and the bun. The meat requires specific attention during the selection process because you need to decide between sliced or mixed in mayonnaise salad. The bun is easy—it is just a bun and you only need to decide how many you want.

You know what sliced meat is, so let's skip that. The mayonnaise salad, though, requires explanation. There are potato and fish salads. Each of these consists of ingredients held together by mayonnaise. Potato salad is a Czech staple served with schnitzel on Christmas Eve, but it is also complements a bun. My favorite is the fish salad because of its bitter aftertaste, which so perfectly counterbalances the bland-mouth effect of a bun. Put a spoonful of bitter fish salad in your mouth, let your tongue absorb the taste, then quickly follow with a bun tear. Chew to mix.

This process, a spoonful of salad followed by a bun bite, is what you will see lunchers performing as they stand around waist-high round tables. There are no chairs at the deli. Find an open spot and mark a section of the table by placing your paper plate down.

Grab hold of your bun like you're holding a baseball bat and start alternating—fish/bun/fish/bun.

Don't expect kindness and handholding at the deli. Delis are for busy people. The staff is efficient, which is mistaken for rudeness by tourists. If you attempt to perform the shoulder shrug, hand-in-the-air thing, it will be returned with exactly the same gesture. The deli is an assembly line for feeding people. The women behind the counter expect you to utter the smallest number of words in the quickest manner possible. Don't bother asking what something is or how much it costs; it will only annoy the staff and the people behind you. Take a chance, point at a salad, grab a bun, and place money down. Move along. Nobody is interested in what you feel like eating or what tastes you feel like avoiding—just pick something, eat it, and get out.

The Czech deli is perfect when you need to eat without going through the whole dance of eating out. It is a big fridge you can open, grab something from it, and eat.

Local Experience: Picnic on Petřín

In 1889 the world was introduced to the Eiffel Tower at the Paris World Fair. Some said it was an abomination and ruined the landscape of Paris, but a group of Czechs belonging to the Club of Czech Tourists were jaw-dropped—they wanted one. When they returned to Prague, they worked the levers and persuaded all the right people. Four short months later, a tower resembling the Eiffel Tower was erected on the top of Petřín Hill.

At only 64 meters high, it is much smaller than its Paris inspiration, but as every proud Czech points out —because it is on the top of a hill, it is higher than the Eiffel Tower.

Besides raising the Petřín Tower above the Eiffel Tower, Petřín Hill is also a nice place for a picnic. The hill is on the left side of the river. To find it, go to an area free from buildings blocking your view (the river is a good place) and look for the Eiffel Tower. Follow the river until you get to the base of the hill.

At the base, you have two options: walk or ride.

If by chance the date is May 1st and you are with your sexual partner and one of you is female, then you need to walk up the hill. The paved path meanders gently back and forth up the hill through a scattered forest of blossoming cherry trees. These trees exploding with the colors of spring have magical powers. On May 1st, and only on May 1st, the cherry tree has the power to pass on its fertility to female humans. To harness this rare power, the female must stand under the tree and receive a passionate kiss from a willing lover. As soon as their lips meet, if the love it true, fertility will rain down from the tree into the woman. Of course, the magical powers have limits; if the female is on the Pill, the potency of the magic is drastically reduced.

If you are not in the mood for romance or walking up a steep 330 meters, you can ride the funicular. Running since 1891, this subway has the rare distinction of being aboveground and traveling uphill. It runs frequently, and as far as I know, nobody got pregnant on it.

The top of the hill is a park with a commanding view of the city. The river cuts through the city with the bridges holding the two sides together like stitches. Prague is said to be the city of a hundred spires; from this perch you can see most of them.

With trees for shade and grass for a bed, go to Petřín for an afternoon picnic and to sneak a snooze. If you did not bring a picnic basket, there are stands selling hand foods like sausages and 'braboraky' (fried mashed potatoes). And, of course, no picnic is complete without beer in plastic cups.

Enjoying the scent of the trees as you lie on your side in the grass, scanning the rooftops of Prague, you are officially on vacation.

Local Experience: Day Trip to Čelákovice

In 1918 Masaryk was the first president of the newly formed Czech Republic. Masaryk is also the name of the second-biggest and oldest train station in Prague.

Since 1845 the Masaryk train station has been used mainly by locals. You will notice as soon as you walk through the large glass entrance there is no McDonald's, there is no information desk, and you want to make sure to hold your nose if you need to use the washroom.

Masaryk station is a hub between Prague and everything east of Prague. Instead of suburbs, the outskirts of Prague consist of small, self-contained towns. Each town has a mayor, church, center square, deli, and, of course, a favorite place for beer and goulash. Masaryk station is for people who work in Prague but have a small town as their home.

By tram, metro, or walking, find the station—it is on the east side of Prague. Walk into the oldest station in Prague, and in front of you will be a crowd of people staring at a table of train times. Ignore that—

it's too complicated. Čelákovice is not the destination, so it will not show up on the table. Depending on the time and day, the destination changes, so to figure out which train you need to get on, you need to know the routes and destinations. Like I said—it's too complicated.

There are six tracks, but starting from the right, the odds are that the train to Čelákovice will be on one of the first three tracks. Four and five are both possible but unlikely. On weekdays the train you need to be on leaves every half hour. Presently, it leaves at :55 and :25. This could change by the time you are here, but only by a maximum of a few minutes—it might be :57 and :27.

You are staring at the first three tracks and the time is :20. There is a train on each track, so which one do you choose? The final step is the most important but also the most difficult. You need to pronounce 'Čelákovice' well enough so that when you ask one of the people standing around, they know what you are saying. Say 'Čelákovice' and they will point to one of the trains. If they slap you, then next time write the name on a piece of paper and show it to them. If there is nobody around that looks pleasant enough to ask, there should be a train conductor in front of every waiting train who will gladly place you on the correct train. You will recognize the train conductors because they look exactly as you would imagine them to look.

Now that you know which train to get on, go look for the ticket booth. Again, it's best to ask because it is located in a completely unpredictable place. For completeness, here are the directions: looking at the trains, turn right and walk down a hallway; turn left at the end and walk all the way down the hallway. The ticket booths are on your left.

You found the ticket booths—good. You need a return ticket to Čelákovice. Say 'Čelákovice' and 'spatecni' (return). It should cost between 80 and 100 CZK. With ticket in hand, find the train and get in. Depending on the time, you will either find a seat easily or you will have to stand—is it rush hour?

The ride is just under 30 minutes. You will pass four stations before arriving in Čelákovice. It is impossible to miss your stop. A voice through the speakers advises what the next stop is, and there is a bright red LED sign indicating the current stop (if train is stopped) and the upcoming stop (if train is moving). Each train station has a large blue banner with the station name. Start paying attention after the 20-minute mark and you will be fine. The stops are Praha

Masarykovo (start), Praha-Vysočany, Praha-Hor.Počernice, Zeleneč, and Čelákovice (end).

As you look out the window and the buildings of Prague fade into grassy fields dotted with rabbits, you realize that you are heading where people do not speak English. At this point you might experience a slight tingle of fear. Let me reassure you, there is nothing to worry about. Czechs do not throw tourists into the river. They will help you if you need help. And no matter where you end up in the Czech Republic, you never have to worry about getting completely lost because all roads lead to Prague. Everybody knows how to get to Prague from where they currently are. So worry not. Be as carefree as the rabbit hunters you see out your window, guns over their shoulders, simply walking and enjoying.

As you intently watch the hunter aim his gun at the bounding rabbit, you might be interrupted by a man in uniform. Sternly, he will reach out his hand. Give him your ticket. He will place your ticket on his ticket reader and, if all is well, stamp it and sign it with his initials. He will give you a nod and a smile as he moves to the next person. You look back—the rabbit is dead, rabbit goulash night.

What Kind of Restaurant Experience Do You Want?

Čelákovice main road is in the shape of an L. When you get off the train and exit the station, you are standing at the top of the L. All the good stuff in Čelákovice is on the bottom, the horizontal part of the L. Walk down the main street until you are forced to turn left. Now you are where the action is

Fortunately, in Čelákovice you do not need to be on guard for tourist traps; odds are you are the only tourist. Feel free to enter any establishment and use a pointing finger to attain a snack at a deli or bakery.

As you walk down Main Street, you will notice stores that resemble 'dollar stores' in that they sell everything from underwear to can openers. Stepping inside one of these stores, you will notice that the proprietor is of Asian descent. These are the Vietnamese, and they run the convenience stores in the Czech Republic. In the 1960s, under the approving eye of the USSR, the Czech Communist government got together with the Vietnamese Communist government and made an exchange. Czech sent Vietnam manufactured goods to assist with the war effort against America, and in return Vietnam sent citizens to Czech. Nobody is certain how this arrangement was supposed to benefit either party, but the USSR is not known to make decisions that improve lives.

There are over 60,000 Vietnamese living in the Czech Republic, and they found themselves a niche. While most Czech-owned convenience stores are closed, the Vietnamese are open. Czechs close at 5 p.m.; Vietnamese stay open until 9 p.m.; Czechs are closed on Sunday; Vietnamese are open. They work hard, and for this reason, the Vietnamese have a good reputation and are respected in Czech.

Find the main square—it has a fountain on one end and a stone-bed creek running through it. The large Communist-built building (you'll recognize it instantly—only a Communist could create such an eyesore) is an international school for business. People visit from all around the world and live in Čelákovice attending classes at the CMC. That's great for them; the benefit to you is that the two main restaurants have English versions of the menu.

On both sides of the square are restaurants, and both have a Pilsner Urquell beer sign. Although both of them have fantastic food, the one called 'BouCZECH' at the foot of the CMC building has a patio right on the square. They also cook well, so sit there and order anything.

Excavation has shown that Čelákovice has had stone structures since the 900s. The first mention of Čelákovice in a book is 1290. So just after the Crusades and around the time Ghengis Khan was wreaking havoc in the East, Čelákovice—sitting smack in the middle of Europe—was busting.

From the square it is a five-minute walk to the church and the hub of late-medieval Čelákovice. The stone church was built around 1300, perched on a small hill. You can imagine the families with their humble homes scattered under its shadow. They would fish in the river and hunt in the woods. Archeologists have discovered pots, jewelry, baskets, weapons, and even canoes. Wild boars roamed the forests and were a constant threat and source of food. Visiting this old church turns words in a history book to a real experience of how people lived. Somebody standing where you are standing was looking at that same church over 700 years ago.

Besides barbarians, enemy armies, and wild boars, the citizens of Čelákovice had to worry about vampires. Čelákovice has the largest vampire graveyard in the world.

In 1966 a homeowner on the outskirts of town needed to expand his house. Digging in his backyard, the shovel struck bone. Thinking it could be a recent murder victim, he called the authorities. Bone experts arrived and determined the skeleton was hundreds of years old, so they called an archeologist. To the homeowner's dismay, his home expansion had to be put on hold until a full excavation could take place.

Čelákovice in the 11th century was a religious and superstitious place. The church at the center of town attests to that, but more evidence is found in the way 11 skeletons were placed in the grave. Their hands and legs were tied, their heads were cut off, and rocks were placed on their bodies. The people who buried them were worried that theses 11 skeletons would return from the dead and attack them.

Like they believed monsters existed in the sea, people believed that vampires existed in Europe. They also believed that if you killed a vampire, then you had to make sure it did not rise from the dead to kill you. Cut off their heads and hands then place rocks on their bodies to hold them firmly underground.

As you walk around Čelákovice and look at the church, consider the fact that there existed a group of people who somehow killed 11 other people because they thought they were vampires. What did the 11 vampires do that was so terrible that they had to be killed and buried in such a manner? Imagine a group of people standing in an empty field, around an unconsecrated hole in the ground far from the holy church, under moonlight, cutting off heads, hands, and feet, and placing heavy rocks on the bodies.

This humble church reminds one of how different an experience people had compared with ours. They worried about vampires; we worry about climate change. What will people looking at this church a thousand years from now worry about?

After a few minutes of pondering this question, you might need to take a long walk along the river. The 'Labe' (Elbe) runs through Čelákovice and is only a few minutes from the church. Not that you should, but if you were to jump into the river, you would be carried with the current north through Germany and tossed into the North Sea.

The train back to Prague leaves every half hour. Go back to the train station, get on the train, and watch out the window as the fields turn back into buildings.

Experience: Street Fast Food

Most Czechs remember where they were when the first McDonald's opened its doors in Prague. Of course, before the grand opening there were months of discussions and debate—it was seen by some as the beginning of the end. Czechs know what it is to be conquered. The Hamburgs did it, the Nazis did it, the Communists did it, and now the Americans were starting to do it. Everybody knows what happens when you let the first McDonald's or Walmart into your town: it won't be long till there is one on every corner.

The push of progress won over those that wanted to keep the American cuisine out. What can little Czech do? Its national animal, the double-tailed lion, has no chance against the persistent pecking of the mighty eagle.

The first McDonald's in Czech had freshly pressed tablecloths and cushions on the seats. You ate off real plates and used stainless steel utensils. It was a night out for the whole family. Parents wanted to see what the Communists had been denying them, and the kids wanted to eat the same food Brad Pitt eats.

It did not take long for the magic to fade. The tablecloths and plates disappeared. Parents went back to their goulash, and kids ate there only because their parents didn't.

As predicted by the conservatives of old Czech culture, McDonald's cracked open the door and let everybody else in. KFC and Burger King are within eyesight of every McDonald's. Pizza Hut tried but failed to catch on—the Czechs' Italian-style light and thin pizza is too entrenched to be usurped by the thick and greasy pizza served by the chain. Subway and Dairy Queen are planning to attack with full force.

But all is not lost. If you are stuck and your only option is McDonald's, you can still experience a little Czech culture. Order a fried cheese sandwich with a pint of Pilsner Urquell beer to wash it down.

You know that if there is a Coca-Cola banner above a street food stand, you are not at a fine-dining establishment. It is even worse when the establishment is sitting in a passageway between two tourist traps. Consider these food stands to be made-for-tourists hotdog stands with rickety walls to keep the flies away. They do not represent the Czech diet any more than cotton candy at Disneyland represents the diet of residents of California. The only time a local would consider eating anything from these food stands is at 4 a.m. when all sense of reason is lost to the influence of one too many.

Wenceslas Square is littered with these fast-food street vendors. I have no idea what the sausages are composed of, but they are unique to these stands. You cannot buy them in a deli. As long as you don't look inside them as you eat, you should be fine.

Instead of succumbing to the glowing Coca-Cola sign and the sound of burgers sizzling, walk a block away from the stand. Look for a ground-floor deli embedded in a 100-year-old building. Chances are this deli has been around for 100 years, and for 100 years, the locals have been buying their meat there. They do not speak English or drink Coca-Cola, but in this deli they know how to make sausages.

Most delis have one or two small round tables at which you can eat your order. Nobody will look at you funny if you order just enough for you—there's nothing wrong with one bun and two slices of ham. (Ham and salami are ordered by weight in decigrams. So if you want 100 grams of ham, then show 10 fingers or say 'decet' ten.)

Buns you buy at the deli contain no preservatives, so they last only a few hours after purchase before they get mushy. That is why in Europe you always see people walking around with pastries—they have to get them every day.

My personal favorite quick meal is a bun with 'palivi' (spicy sausage). You have a bun in one hand and sausage in the other. Bite the sausage and chew out the juice then follow quickly with a bite of the bun. If timed correctly, the bite down on the bun will be dry in the mouth, but as the bun is compressed flat, it absorbs the sauces of the sausage. The airy crispness of the bun combined with the spicy mush of the juice creates every sensation your mouth can experience. You might look like a performing monkey alternating your bun hand and your sausage hand, but at least you are not one of the fools a block away eating at a rickety hot dog stand.

How to Get to the Restaurant

Buying a public transport ticket is a daunting task. There are more buttons on the ticket machine than in the cockpit of a 747.

To simplify things, the machine is broken up into zones and times. So you can get a ticket that is valid for 20 minutes and two zones or a ticket that is valid for 90 minutes and four zones.

When you come to the machine, you should have an idea where you are going and how long it should take to get there. Try to estimate the number of stations and the duration of your trip to your destination. When I don't know, I press the 90-minute button; in 90 minutes you can easily get anywhere in Prague. It is better to overpay than try to save a few korunas and then argue with the transport authority.

Validating the ticket is a two step process. First, you buy the ticket then you need to validate it. At the entrance of the metro zone and inside the buses and trams are little yellow boxes. Insert the ticket into the box to get it time-stamped.

If you have your mobile phone, an easy way to buy a ticket is to send an SMS to the number 902 06 26. In the message you can type 'DPT32', 'DPT24', 'DPT110', or 'DPT310', depending on how many minutes you need for the ticket to be valid. Within seconds your phone account will be debited, and you will receive an SMS metro ticket. If you are stopped by a public transport authority, simply show them the SMS. The ticket is valid for the entire Prague transit system (metro, tram, bus), and it is valid for a child or adult—even dog.

The public transport authority is usually a plainclothes man with a badge who appears from out of nowhere. Suddenly, a man is standing in front of you and mumbling something you do not understand. Next, he will gesture down towards his crotch—don't be scared. He wants you to notice his round red badge. The badge indicates that he has the legal right to see your ticket, so show him your ticket. If you are without a ticket, one of two things will happen: (1) You're cute and he is in a good mood, so he lets you go with a few more mumbles that you do not understand. (This is very unlikely—these guys deal with tourists pleading ignorance all the time.) (2) He wants to see your passport, and you are forced to pay a 800 CZK fine. I have seen people run away from these men with badges, but I do not recommend this third option since it is safer and simpler to make sure you have a valid ticket.

Take the Metro

The metro system is easy to understand. There are three lines: red, green, and yellow. It does not matter which line you start on—you can always get to any other one. All three lines go through the center of town.

Walking down into the metro station, you will be faced with two options: either stand on the left platform or the right platform. At the center and above each platform is an easy-to-understand map. It lists all the stations for the line. The circled and bold station is the one where you presently are. To the right of the circled station are the stations that the right platform metro will take you. To the left of the circled station are the stations that the left platform will take you.

If you need an overall picture of the entire metro system, there is a metro map encased in glass somewhere on the platform. It will show you where you are and which stations you need to get to in order to make a crossover to another line. The crossover stations are Florence, Muzeum, and Mustek.

Metro trains run from 5 a.m. till midnight in two- to three-minute intervals during peak hours and in four- to 10-minute intervals in the off hours. Each station has a digital clock that indicates how much time has passed since the last train left.

Take the Tram

The tram is an important method of transportation in Prague city center. It is easy to use because it's at street level, so you do not need to ride up and down stairs like the metro. (The Prague metro is really deep underground because during the Cold War metro stations were supposed to double as nuclear war shelters, although recently it has been shown that there was not enough ventilation to survive for more than a few days.) Trams can sprint through the city because they have the right-of-way above everything —cars, pedestrians, and even old ladies. And they are frequent; you never have to stand at a stop for long because a tram comes along every few minutes.

Locals use the trams as naturally as monkeys use their tails. Instead of walking a few blocks, they

How to Get to the Restaurant

simply hop into a tram, ride the few blocks, and hop out.

Unfortunately, trams are not that natural for tourists. The problem is figuring out which tram goes where. Trams twist and turn through Prague streets with no apparent logic, but because trams are so convenient, you should at least try and go for a ride. Here is some advice:

Each tram is identified by a number. Written on the side of the tram are the stops the tram makes. But that will tell you nothing—especially since you have only 30 seconds to read it before the tram leaves again. Plus, in most cases, the names have nothing to do with the destination—you will not find a Charles Bridge station.

Once you figure out where you want to go, you need to find out where you are. Every tram stop has a red pole with a little bulletin board. On the board are columns of paper sheets; each individual sheet describes the route of an individual tram. Five sheets of paper means five trams use the stop. Each paper will have the tram number and a list of the stops.

Here is the most important tip and the one that took me a while to notice: the bold station is the one where you currently are. The stations below the bold one are where the tram is going next, and the stations above the bold are where the tram is coming from.

Using the tram map, you should be able to hop your way from tram to tram and get to almost anywhere in the city.

Daytime trams run from 4:30 a.m. till midnight in eight- to 10-minute intervals (eight to 15 minutes on weekends). Night trams run from 00:30 a.m. till 4:30 a.m. in 40-minute intervals.

Take a Taxi

Taxi drivers have a bad reputation in Prague—they deserve it. In 2010 a study was done to determine how much taxi drivers charge tourists for a ride from the airport to city center. Half the taxi drivers overcharged. A taxi ride from the airport to city center should cost around 600 CZK. A few taxi drivers charged the undercover tourists 5000 CZK.

After many complaints from tourists, the city started to listen and implemented changes to rectify the problem. Now at the airport you will notice a special place for official Prague taxis. These taxis have a fixed price for common destinations in the city center. There is no more haggling or surprises; each taxi stop has a sign with destinations and prices. These designated taxi stops describing how much you should pay from one destination to another are scattered throughout the city. When the taxi arrives, confirm the price and you should be safe from being ripped off.

Of course, if you hail your own taxi from who knows where at 3 a.m., then you are at the taxi driver's mercy—enter at your own risk. A ride in the district of Prague is around 28 CZK/km ($1.30 USD). The boarding fee is 40 CZK ($1.65 USD). Waiting is 6 CZK/1 min ($0.25 USD). Do a quick estimate of the number of kilometers from where you are and where you are heading. If the price for the taxi ride is plus or minus 25 percent, then you are fine. If the price is 200 percent more, then I would get another taxi. Worst-case scenario, if the taxi driver is arguing and asking for 1000 CZK, give him 300 CZK and let him discuss the rest with your hotel's reception.

Since the prices from the airport to city center are fixed, you do not need to tip from the airport. But if you are in a giving mood, 10 percent is an acceptable tip. Try to round it off to the nearest 20 CZK or 50 CZK. If the bill is 280 CZK, pay the man 300 CZK. If the bill is 660 CZK, pay 700 CZK.

Walk

Prague city center is small enough that you can walk from anywhere to anywhere. Walking from one side of city center to the other side takes about an hour. So if you need to build up a hunger before a meal, then walk there. Prague is an interesting city with narrow alleys and ancient buildings to keep your eyes busy. In the center, a lot of the roads are for pedestrians only. Where cars are permitted, the traffic is sparse because the roads are narrow and congested with people.

The only thing you need to be warned about while walking around is that trams (city trains) have the right-of-way over pedestrians. You have to move out of their way. They will not stop and let you cross, and they will not wait until you are out of the way before they start moving. It is your responsibility to be out of their way. A tram driver loves nothing more than to find a confused tourist standing on the tracks—he will ring the bell, speed up, and watch your eyes bulge as you jump out of the way.

The roads are cobblestone, and the older the road the more dangerous it is. Hundreds of years ago every rock was handpicked and hand placed. Each rock is different, so each gap is unique. I do not have the stats, but I am certain Prague hospitals receive plenty of patients with sprained ankles. Prague sidewalks are not designed for high heels. Wear comfortable and padded shoes.

Is Prague Safe?

You know what happens after reading a book about diseases—you believe you might have most of them. The same thing happens when you read about Prague in the Internet forums. Rarely do tourists create an account and go through the trouble of writing that their trip was positive. Most tourists will create an account to 'warn' against a terrible incident that happened to them. It seems that 1 percent of bad incidents make up 99 percent of the forum posts. A few hours on the forums and you might begin to believe that Prague is backwards and Eastern (Communist East not Asian East).

Because you are reading this in English, I assume you are from a 'Western country' (American West not Cuban West). Czech is a small country, and most Westerners don't know where Czech is on the map; their best guess is that it is an Eastern European country. For them, it is difficult to differentiate between Czech, Romania, Bulgaria, or Ukraine; to them, they all belong to the mental category of Eastern and Communist. The image is the same for all Eastern countries—grey, factory smoke, dirty, criminal, corrupt.

Let me assure you that Czech has become as Western as any Western country. It has a Communist history, but that was 20 years ago. Czech existed in a Communist bubble, so when the Communists were kicked out, Czech burst into the modern world.

In terms of your safety and how Czechs behave towards their fellow man, it is no different than in your hometown. There is no need to learn self-defense or drag around a backpack full of survival gear. Do you tape your wallet to your belly when you go to the corner stop in your hometown? There is no need to do that in Prague either.

All the negative experiences I have read about in the forums are experiences that could happen anywhere. Somebody feels they paid too much for salami, so they are warning how they got ripped off in Prague. Yes, you can get ripped off in Prague, but you can get ripped off anywhere in the world.

I am not preaching. I am trying to save you worry and wasted effort. I live in Prague and take exactly the same precautions you take in your hometown—nothing more.

How a Pickpocket Picks Pockets

The odds are in your favor that your pockets will not be picked. The chances are so small that you should not even worry about it. Use common sense—don't have a hundred dollar bill dangling from your back pocket and you will be fine.

But pickpocketing does occur in Prague—as it does in every tourist city. Tourists are easily spotted and they are easily distracted. Tourist's eyeballs are everywhere other than around their own bodies. All their attention is on the slightest distraction (a monkey playing a clarinet) while completely ignoring the stranger's hand in their pants.

Of course, you are smarter than that. You will be careful and alert, and anybody within a one-meter radius will be suspect; you will watch them closely. That is what everybody thinks, yet pickpocketing still occurs.

To give you an idea how pickpocketing works, here is an example.

Tomas and Franta are pickpockets. Their specialty is smart phones. After a pleasant breakfast, they head to Wenceslas Square.

The famous square is a tourist hot spot, bustling with the lost who are showcasing their smart phones as they follow the little arrow on the screen. Tomas and Franta sit down on a park bench and wait. No rush, they have all day. One success per day is enough to make the day worth it. They might wait for hours and then follow a target for a few blocks. If everything is not perfect, they abort and wait for somebody else.

A young woman with an 'I heart Prague' T-shirt walks by. She has buds in her ears and is selecting music on her iPhone. Tomas and Franta get up and follow her. She picks her songs and places the iPhone in her jacket pocket. Tomas takes note of the pocket on her left side. Franta picks up his pace and walks ahead of her, pulling out a map of Prague. He stops at the intersection and stares, confused, at his map. When she approaches him, he starts moving his lips like he is asking her a question. She takes off her headphones and starts to explain that she does not know. In that instant, Tom walks by on her left side. Franta nods to her, says thanks, continues to look at his map, and slowly walks off. She puts her headphones back in her ears and is surprised to hear nothing.

Pickpocketing is rare. It will not happen to you, but it does happen. The above is just one variation but there are others. Unfortunately, there is nothing you can do to protect yourself—you are up against pros that make their living separating you from your phone. If you are targeted, they will follow you all day just to get that perfect opportunity to snatch it. My advice? Don't worry about it; it won't happen to you.

The Grandmothers of Prague – Keep Away— They Will Attack

Almost as ancient at the masonry in the castle walls are the grandmothers that walk the streets of Prague.

They have waded through hell and survived: two world wars, Communism, revolution, and most recently, the heartless feeding frenzy of capitalism. They are bitter and they do not like you.

If one hobbles towards you—get out of the way. Step aside, give her the entire sidewalk, and let her pass. If she is impatiently waiting at the bus stop, let her board the bus first. Mistakenly move ahead of her and you will find yourself on the ground with a grocery-bag-shaped bruise on your forehead.

You might think that you are seeing the same person all over town, but what you are actually witnessing is the Prague army of grandmothers. They wear the same dress, and they all have the same mission: They must gather a daily ration of four buns (one to feed the pigeons), a sausage, a stick of butter, and a bottle of fresh milk. They must not overpay. They must put it all into two grocery bags, and most importantly, they must get back home before 11 a.m.

They will stop at nothing to complete this mission. They will push ahead of you in line, they will haggle with the cashier over a couple korunas, they will walk in the middle of sidewalk, and they will mumble loudly if you impede them in the slightest. Their canes turn into swift swords with the slightest provocation. Ask them the time and you risk a lash across the backside.

Fortunately, members of the grandmothers army are easy to spot. Here are a few things to look for:

- Old, very old.

- A little hunched over, needs to crane her neck to see forward.

- Their uniform is a one-piece dress that stops just above the ankles and has short sleeves, is light grey, and is covered with little blue flower designs. It is clean but looks dirty. Grandmothers like the one-piece because it is warm in the winter and airy in the summer. The dress also creates a natural pouch between the knees when peeling potatoes. On cooler days, they will wear an itchy-looking sweater with big buttons on the front.

- They wear a babushka—a piece of cloth similar to what old men pull out of their pockets and blow their nose with. Grandmothers put a babushka on their head, tie it under their chin, and let it drop to a point down their backs. Nobody knows why they wear them.
- Always in a hurry, but moving very slow.
- Two reusable cloth grocery bags, one in each hand.
- They walk in the exact center of the sidewalk and are not concerned with human obstacles. They will push and complain their way through any crowd—could be a bunch of giddy schoolgirls or a rowdy pack of football fanatics.
- Wield a cane or a crutch.
- They feed chunks of bun to street pigeons. Their wrinkled faces are frowned, and they do not seem to be receiving any pleasure from it. They appear to do it out of some kind of forced duty—a burden bestowed upon them by an unknown master.
- They will force their way through the crowded bus to the door long before the bus stops at the station. Anybody who does not get out of their

way will get stern looks, head shaking, and undecipherable mumbles.

Be careful. They do not mind if you take a picture, just make sure to stay out of their way. They need to get those groceries home before 11 a.m.

You Are at the Restaurant

You approach the restaurant door and pull on the handle. The door opens with a squeak and you walk in. The first thing you see is two men holding each other by the neck and rolling on the table. The bartender is holding a shotgun in his hands and is pointing it at the ceiling about to pull the trigger. A frightened waitress is hiding under a table, and a wide-eyed old man is swinging off a chandelier.

Suddenly you hear a whizzing sound and a pfffffffffft. You look to your right and see an angry man with his arm extended—you quickly conclude he has just thrown something. You feel nothing, but you hear the beer mug explode across your forehead. Your head is bleeding but you don't care because you're knocked out cold, lying flat on the restaurant floor.

The above scenario is extremely unlikely. It is one in a million. But even so, in Prague the tradition is that when a couple walks into a restaurant that sells beer, the man enters first. In most cultures, the gentleman offers the courtesy of opening the door for the lady. In Prague, the courtesy is that the gentleman walks in first to ensure that he is the target of flying beer mugs.

You Want a Beer

Czech beer is world famous. Czech people enjoy beer —they really enjoy beer. The Czech Republic is the world leader of the number of liters consumed per year per capita. And it's not just a couple percentage points, Czechs are far ahead with 158 liters per person (that is equivalent to all citizens drinking a half-liter pint every day of the year). Ireland is next with 131 liters per person, and the U.S. is ridiculously behind at 82 liters.

A possible reason for this lead is the taste of Czech beer, but a more economical explanation is the price of Czech beer. It is one of the least expensive drinks you can buy—less than a Coke, less than a coffee, and even less than a glass of water. Because beer is such an important aspect of Czech culture, the government does not dare tax it too heavily. Any government daring to even suggest increasing the tax on beer would be chased out of city hall by men with pitchforks and grannies with brooms.

You Are at the Restaurant

Ordering a beer is probably the easiest thing to do in Prague. Everybody just assumes that you want one, so all it takes is a nod, a raised finger, or mouthing 'ano' (yes) when the waiter looks at you from across the room.

As soon as you are settled at your table, a waiter will step up and say "Netco na pit?" (Something to drink?) All you have to say is 'pivo' (beer). Don't worry about brand, type, strength, or size—it has all been taken care of for you. Every restaurant has a default beer, the beer you get when you do not want to specify details. Depending on the restaurant, the brand and the strength vary, but in all local restaurants it is served in a half-litre mug while in tourist restaurants the default is a smaller third-litre mug.

Ordering your second beer is even simpler than the first. Right after your finish your last swig, the waiter will notice your empty mug. He will come to your table and, reaching for the empty mug, say 'Ještě?' (Another one?) The slightest nod or mouthed 'ano' (yes) will do.

After the second beer, he will notice your beer is almost done from behind the bar. Nod your head and your beer is on its way.

After the third beer, the waiter will take initiative and bring beers automatically. He assumes, and in most cases he is correct, that you want another beer. Being a professional, he times the next beer so that it arrives exactly at the moment you swallow the last drop. Most of the time he gets it exactly right, but sometimes he miscalculates and arrives a little early. Because he does not want to leave the new beer without taking the empty mug back with him, he will wait for you to finish. Pour the last bit down quickly and move on to the next.

The problem with this process is getting him to stop. The trick is to not drink your beer below the 30 percent-remaining mark. As soon as you get below that mark, his radar turns on and he starts to plan the next beer. At the 30 percent mark, tell him you want to 'zaplatit' (pay the bill). Now your challenge is counting korunas after eight beers.

Be adventurous and go beyond the default beer. Here is all you need to know:

- There are six main brands of beer: Pilsner Urquell, Gambrinus, Staropramen, Budvar, Kozel, and Radegast.
- The alcohol strength is indicated by a number: 10 (~3.5%) is a weak beer and 13 (>5%) is a strong

beer. For example, Pilsner Urquell is a 12 beer and Staropramen is an 11 beer. You can order a beer based on alcohol level, so if you just say 'dvanác' (12), then you will normally get a Pilsner Urquell. Technically, this number is not an alcohol-level indicator. The number indicates the amount of malt used in the brewing processes. But because there is usually a correlation between the amount of malt used and the alcohol level, it can be used to estimate alcohol level.

- There are two sizes of beer mugs: the popular .5 liter (even cans are .5 liter) and the smaller .3 liter. If you do not specify what you want, then you will get the .5 liter by default (unless you're at a tourist spot where the default is .3 liter).

- It is considered lowbrow to drink more than one type of beer at a restaurant. You look like a desperate alcoholic drinking for the alcohol and not appreciating the taste of your favorite beer. Pick a brand and stick with it the whole night.

- There is nothing wrong with mixing a light and dark beer into one mug. Say 'zezani' and you will receive the lightness of golden beer mixed with the heaviness of dark beer. There is no way to accurately describe the taste—think OREO.

There is one more detail that you should know. In English, if you want one beer, you say 'one beer, please'. If you have more than one beer, then you add an 's' to the end of 'beer'—'five beers please'. Simple, right? But in Czech it is more complicated than that. Here is a quick guide to follow, depending on how much you enjoy beer. (Notice how the word for beer —'pivo'—changes depending on the number of beers):

1 beer = jedno pivo, 2 beers = dvě piva, 3 beers = tři piva, 4 beers = čtyři piva, 5 beers = pět piv. And just in case you need to know ... 11 beers = 11 piv.

Turkish Coffee

The problem with drinking beer in the afternoon is that it makes you tired. And if you are not napping, you are probably babbling nonsense until the alcohol wears off. The Renaissance, the great emergence of human intellect and creative progress, started around the same time as the first coffeehouse opened in the year 1554 in Constantinople.

When people started to sip the black bean instead of guzzle dark lager, the world instantly got a lot smarter. Instead of sitting around and complaining about how the king is doing everything wrong, energized by caffeine, people began to be more productive. Books were written and discussed, marble was chipped into an idealized reflection of man, and devious smiles were painted on the innocent. And, most importantly, it was discovered that the Earth is not the center of the universe. A man full of beer can't even comprehend that he is not the center of the universe.

Prague, with the highest consumption of beer per capita, can lead you to assume that you will be visiting a city full of semi-awake, self-righteous, perpetually complaining dullards. Yes, you will come across a few of these, but fortunately, to offset the ill effects of beer, locals drink very strong Turkish coffee.

Turkish coffee is finely ground coffee that only partially dissolves. It is strong and hot—a coffee to be sipped. It is served with a biscuit and a shot glass of water. Remove any lingering tastes in your mouth by washing them down with the water before starting the coffee. You are done when only a thick layer of coffee mud remains at the bottom of the cup.

As in most European cities, locals love to idle around on sidewalk patios and lubricate their conversations with strong coffee. Unlike with beer, where the conversation quality suffers with time, coffee allows the conversation to persist intelligently well past the one-hour mark.

When I arrived in Prague in 2006, you could not get brewed coffee anywhere. The choice was either Turkish coffee or espresso. People did not walk around with a coffee thermos or drink it on the train. Cars did not come standard with coffee holders. For these reasons, Starbucks was late to penetrate the Czech market. Czechs had strong ties to their coffee and how they drank it. The whole idea of a half liter of coffee 'to go' was completely foreign. It still is foreign but Starbucks continues to push. Five years ago there were no Starbucks; now there are eight. Not surprisingly, some Czechs take offense and consider Starbucks a bigger attack on tradition than the burger.

Kofola

During Communism it was almost impossible to get a drink of Coca-Cola in Czechoslovakia. Coca-Cola was created by capitalist pigs, so the government provided its citizens the service of protecting them from the sugary black drink. Of course people wanted it, but the government was not asking them.

Then in 1959 the government had a problem. They had too much caffeine left over from their processing of roasting coffee. Because they could not simply sell their surplus of caffeine in the open market like the evil people did, they had to find another Communist-friendly use for it. A group of chemists, probably craving Coke, mixed the ingredients they had and added the surplus caffeine to make a brownish, almost black syrup. Add water and bingo! Coca-Cola in Czechoslovakia.

Kofola became an instant success. Kids guzzled it down on hot days, and parents used it to flavor their alcohol. Everybody older than 40 has fond memories of their childhood and how Kofola was always right there at every milestone in life—just like in the sappiest American Coke commercials.

The taste is unique and does not taste like Coke. At first, it tastes a touch like licorice, but only if you are used to drinking Coke. After a few drinks, the licorice taste goes away. I would compare the taste more to root beer than to Coke. Whatever your first impression, let me warn you that it is an acquired taste, so do not give up on it. Keep trying it until you enjoy it, just like the citizens of Communism did.

Czechs and Slovaks acquired the taste because they had no choice, but it is a popular drink even today. Kofola is stacked right alongside Coke and

Pepsi in every store. In 1989, when the global markets were allowed into Czechoslovakia, Coke and Pepsi arrived and flooded the market with advertisements and products. They had the bonus that people were eager to consume anything and everything as long as it was not Communist made. People drank Coke just because it was American and it was denied to them. But slowly, as the novelty of America has faded and pride in Czech-made products has increased, Kofola has made a comeback. In Czech, Kofola is very close behind Coke in yearly sales; in Slovakia Kofola sells more than Coke. It probably helps sales that in most bars and restaurants, Kofola is offered on tap. So if you need a break from beer, grab a stool at the bar and order yourself a cold pint of Kofola.

Water Is Not Free

You might expect that when you order fries with your 'řízek' (schnitzel), the waiter will bring a bottle of ketchup to the table. Unfortunately, that is not going to happen. If you want ketchup, you need to ask for it and pay for it. It's not that the restaurant is trying to squeeze every dime out of you; it's just that ketchup is considered an extra.

Here are a few other things that you might think are free but are not:

- Water. If you want water, you need to pay for it. They are not going to bring an ice-filled jug of water with glasses. When you ask for water, they are going to ask 'Neparliva nebo parlivá?' ('Without bubbles or with bubbles?'—non-carbonated or carbonated.) If you want normal water, say 'neparlivá'. The waiter will bring you a little bottle of water and a glass. He will open the bottle in front of you and pour the glass half-full. Refills are not free, and it is also more expensive than a half liter of beer.

- Ketchup. There are no ketchup bottles on the tables. Remember, if you want ketchup, you need to ask for it—even when you order fries. The ketchup is served in a little dish. Do not be gluttonous with the ketchup. If you run out and you still have a few fries left, you will have to order another little dish of ketchup.

- Coffee Refills. I have never been to a restaurant in Prague that served brewed coffee. It is always an espresso in the little dollhouse cup that you hold with your index finger and thumb. It's not coffee; it's more like a strong shot of caffeine.

Refills are not free, and it is also more expensive than a half liter of beer.

• Buns. When you order soup, it will arrive with a basket full of fresh buns. Go ahead—eat all the buns you want. But when it's time for the bill, be prepared to answer the waiter's question: 'Kolik hosky?' ('How many buns?') You can try lying and say that you had two buns when you really had three, but because they cost only a few korunas each, it is probably not worth the sleepless nights of guilt.

• Tartar Sauce. It is a mandatory condiment for a few popular Czech dishes—fried cheese ('smažený sýr') and fried cauliflower ('smažený kvetak'), for example. Were you to be offered these dishes at a Czech's house, it would come with tartar sauce automatically. But at a restaurant you need to ask and pay for it.

• Salt and Pepper. Just in case you were wondering—they are free.

Your Knife and Fork Speak to the Waiter

Even if you can't speak a word of Czech, you can tell your waiter: (1) you are not done eating even though there is only one dumpling remaining and you have

You Are at the Restaurant

not touched your food in 20 minutes, and (2) you are done eating even though you have not touched the meat and have eaten only one dumpling.

The secret is the position of your knife and fork on the plate. This is important to learn because it prevents embarrassing situations in which the waiter reaches for your plate even though you are not done or does not take your plate away when you are done.

To let your waiter know that you are taking a rest from eating and that you do not want him to take the plate away, place the knife in the five o'clock position and the fork in the seven o'clock position.

To let your waiter know that you are done and want him to take the plate away, put the fork and knife in the three o'clock position.

Why do beer drinkers keeping mentioning a castrated bull?

A bull paces back and forth behind a gate. It flares its nostrils, digs its hoofs through the ground, bucks and pushes. Open the gate and get out of the way because he is about to explode out of there. This is a classic image of a bull—big, strong, ready to strike, and very horny.

The word you will hear most at any local beer pub in Czech is 'vole'. Direct translation? Castrated bull. It is the Czech 'fuck' word and it wields similar powers.

The same men sit around the same table at the same time every day. They talk about the same things over and over and over again. The orator will pound his fist on the table and intersperse his speech with 'vole' at the beginning, middle, and end. The others at the table will react with laughter. He either just described how the government screwed him, or he undisputedly proved that somebody is an idiot. Both of these trains of discussion require many instances of 'vole' for a successful delivery.

Like 'fuck', 'vole' can be used as a noun, verb, and adjective. 'Vole' can be used for the guy who just said something stupid like, 'KFC tastes better than goulash'—'Ty vole' (translation: 'You stupid idiot'). If somebody orders 10 dumplings with their goulash, you will hear a whistle and a 'Tyyy vooole' (translation: 'Wow! That's a lot of dumplings, you stupid idiot'). If a guy shouts out 'vole' and waves his arm at another guy who is looking around, it means, 'Hey! I am over here'.

A magical transformation happens after the fourth round of Czech beers. Everybody else becomes a

You Are at the Restaurant

stupid idiot, and so the use of 'vole' drastically increases. All stories involve somebody doing something stupid. As the stories are told, the listeners around the table shake their heads, slowly raise their beers towards their mouths, and mumble 'Ty vole'.

Why castrated bull? I have no idea. There is nothing special about a castrated bull. It doesn't do anything. Cows in heat pass by, but the bull does nothing—it just stands there like a stupid idiot and chews grass.

Zaplatíme (Ready to Pay)

The worst part of the evening—paying.

When you want the bill, you say, 'Zaplatíme' ('Ready to pay').

Some local restaurants do not have a cash register, so you will not get a printed receipt. During your meal, the waiter was making marks on a little piece of paper that he left at your table. Every time you ordered something he made another mark on the paper. A beer is usually indicated with a line—five beers is four lines with a cross through it.

When you are ready to pay, he will add everything up in front of you. There is nothing you can do but trust him. Some local restaurants do not even have a piece of paper. At the end of the night, the waiter will ask you to refresh his memory with what you ate and how many beers you had.

Although almost all tourist restaurants accept credit cards, almost no local restaurants do, so bring cash unless you are ready to wash dishes.

Thanks to the collapse of Communism, tipping has become the norm. There are still Czechs who are sticking to the old ways and do not tip at all. Most, though, will at least round to the nearest 10 CZK—a final bill for 292 CZK will earn the waiter 8 CZK. The waiter will not be happy, but he will not be surprised either.

You, however, a tourist accustomed to tipping, should tip around 10 percent. For an average meal, round to the nearest 20 or 100 CZK. A meal for two with a couple beers will cost around 270 CZK. Give the waiter 300 CZK and he will be happy.

It is not customary to leave a pile of bills and coins on the table. When the waiter comes to collect, he will write the number on a piece of paper. Give him the money, including the tip, and say 'Děkuji' ('Thank you').

How to Talk to a Waiter That Does Not Understand English

The reason most tourists do not venture far from the tourist zones is because of language. There are about 10 million people who speak Czech in the world, and 99 percent of them live in the Czech Republic. So if you do not live in the Czech Republic, there is no point learning to speak Czech. Fortunately, all you need is a few words, and you are ready to dine like a local.

Besides being a Slavic language with inherent difficulties for English speakers, Czech has the added twist of having R's that are insanely unpronounceable. The ř is a distinct sound unique to the Czech language. The sound is produced by touching the tip of the tongue to the roof of the mouth, and then, by blowing air, you allow the tongue to slap against the palate a few times. Children need to practice this sound as part of their language lessons. Veteran nonnative Czech speakers give themselves away instantly by the way they pronounce their slapping ř.

To say 'Hi' to the bell boy and 'Thank you' to the waiter is easy enough—'Ahoj' and 'Děkuji' (no R's). The problems start when you try to string a few words together. There is a good reason why Czech is considered the Rolls Royce of languages. It has many intricacies and rules that can make your head spin even before you have your first mug of pivo (beer).

Fortunately the Czech people realize their language is difficult and are not disappointed when you try and fail to sputter out a few words. They will smile and correct you. You will say it wrong again. Fortunately, I have never heard of an incident where someone was kicked out of restaurant for mispronouncing 'svíčková na smetaně, knedlík' (beef sirloin with dumplings and vegetable cream sauce).

If you are visiting the Czech Republic for a few days or a few weeks, there is no point trying to learn the language. But a couple words and phrases are handy to know.

The Czech language is a phonic language, meaning that words are spelled the way they sound. That makes it easy to read Czech words if you know the sounds of the letters. Most Czech letters sound similar to English letters. The only significant exceptions are that the Czech 'y' sounds like the English 'e'; the Czech 'j' sounds like the English 'h', and the Czech 'e' sounds like English 'eh'.

There is no point memorizing the different sound effects accents have on the letters. They make such a

You Are at the Restaurant

small difference to the sound that for all practical purposes you can ignore them.

To hear how a word sounds, you can write (or paste) it into Google Translator and it will say the word for you.

Regardless of your ability to slap your tongue against the roof of your mouth, you do not need to be afraid of entering into a local restaurant because you will do just fine with hand gestures and pointing. But with a few words you can surprise the waiter and simplify the experience for both of you.

Here is a standard scenario in a Czech restaurant. Learn these few words and you will be acting like a local in no time.

It is 11 a.m. and you just returned from a march up to the Prague Castle. You are starving and annoyed with the crowded streets full of tourists, so you break off into a narrow, empty street. You look for a beer sign hanging over the door. Walking a block, you find a glowing green Pilsner Urquell sign. You push the old door and walk inside.

Waiter: Dobry den. (Good day.)
You: Dobry den.

Waiter points to an empty table and you sit down.

> Waiter: Jídelní lístek? (Do you want a menu?)
> You: Ano, prosim. (Yes, please.)
> Waiter: Něco k pití? (Something to drink?)
> You: Pivo. (Beer.)

The waiter leaves. He returns with a menu and your beer. He makes a little mark on a piece of paper, places it on your table, and leaves. You look over the menu and find the section called 'minotuvy' (done) and scan for the word 'knedlik' (dumplings). Using the advice of this book, you randomly pick one of the meat, sauce, and dumplings offers. The waiter returns.

> Waiter: Máte vybráno? (Have you decided?)
> You: Ano, dam si ... [Just point to your selection—don't even try to pronounce it.] (Yes, I will have ...]

The waiter acknowledges with a smile, picks up the little piece of paper, makes another mark, and places the paper back on the table. He takes the menu from you and leaves. You lean back and drink your beer. It is not as carbonated as you are used to so no burp, but the .5 pint fills a bladder quickly. You get up and approach the waiter.

You: Kde je toaleta? (Where is the bathroom?)

The waiter points to a door with a picture of a little boy sitting on a toilet. You take care of business and return to the table. You ordered from the 'minotovy' (done) section, so your food arrives quickly. The waiter places the plate in front of you and picks up your empty beer glass.

Waiter: Ešte jedno pivo? (Another beer?)

You: Ne Dik. (No thanks.)

Waiter: Dobrou chuť. (Good appetite.) [It is a Czech tradition to wish an eater a good appetite before he begins the meal. When people sit around a table, everybody says 'dobrou chut' before they start eating.]

Your plate has five dumplings, beef, and a white creamy sauce—you ordered the Czech classic 'svickova'. Because this is your third meat, sauce, and dumpling dish in Prague, you have mastered the soaking properties of the dumpling and are able to finish the meal with a perfectly clean plate. You smack your lips and place the knife and fork at the three o'clock position on the plate. The waiter arrives.

You: Zaplatím. (I am ready to pay.)

The waiter nods and picks up the little piece of paper. He adds up the beer and the meal and writes 85. He shows you the number, and you pull out a 100 korunas bill and hand it to him.

> You: To je dobre. (That is good—keep the change.)
> Waiter: Dik, hesky den. (Thanks, have a nice day.)

The waiter takes your plate and leaves. As you walk towards the door, you pass by the waiter.

> Waiter: Na shledanou. (Bye.)
> You: Na shledanou.

Conversation Topics While You Eat

Main Course: A Brief History of Prague

I am not a professor of history. I did not spend years in the library reading dusty books. I have never entered the catacombs under the city in search of artifacts. But I have read a few books about Prague, and I have listened to old men tell their stories. I have read building plaques and visited museums. Unfortunately, as with all memories, I do not remember every conversation or exact dates, but I am certain of the basic plot.

Here is the story of Prague told by someone who lives in the city and experiences its history every day.

No More Mammoths, Prague is Born

Under the Prague castle there are bricks that date back to 885AD. They were part of a fort located at the highest point in Prague. Below, in the valley by the river, were houses and a market—baby Prague.

Before that, way before that, mammoths grazed Prague. Of course, they are all long gone, hunted down by the meat-loving ancestors of modern meat-loving Czechs. Visit the National Museum if you want to see a full-sized replica of the beast.

Charles IV Builds a Bridge and Paints the Town Gold

Not much happened between the founding of Prague around 900AD and 1350AD. There were battles as kings and princes fought over patches of land; castles were built and then they were destroyed. Homes were built by one generation and then destroyed by the next. Men were killed, women raped, and children sold as slaves—the usual 1000AD kind of stuff.

Baby Prague expanded by beating and killing its neighbors until they surrendered their cows and tomatoes. As in hundreds of other hill and valley cities around the world, humans killed, abused, and loved each other all on the same day. These days rolled one onto the next with not much happening.

Suddenly, though, everything changed when Charles IV took over. What Steve Jobs did for Apple, Charles did for Prague.

Just before Charles arrived, Prague managed to build itself into a cute little city. There were a looming castle on the hill and a bustling town square in the valley below. The newly built Judith Bridge over the river connected the castle with the city.

Through no-doubt dubious and double-crossing tactics, Charles IV managed to become king of Bohemia. This by itself was no small feat, but the feather in his cap was that he managed to become the emperor of the Holy Roman Empire at the same time. Charles decided to settle in Prague. When he did, real estate prices shot up, and the humble little city became the third largest in Europe.

Charles worked hard for his crown. He did not spend his days laughing at the jester. He was a scholar. To quench his thirst for knowledge, he built the first university in Europe. To please the all-seeing man in the sky, he built the Gothic Saint Vitus Cathedral, which has become a great place for group photos. And finally, after a flood toppled the rickety Judith Bridge, Charles commissioned the sturdy Charles Bridge.

The city became the Golden City thanks to Charles.

Jan Hus Burns at the Stake, 20 Years of War, and More Good Times

All parties must come to an end. Usually it is when the beer runs out or somebody suffers a black eye. In Prague, the party ended when Charles was too old to wake up. After the somber parade, Charles's son Wenceslaus IV settled down on his father's throne. If he assumed it would all run on cruise control, it must have disappointed him when Jan Hus started preaching.

Today you can see a statue of Jan Hus in the center of Old Town Square. He is standing proud and tall. Behind him are his followers—mostly peasants with pitchforks.

In the 1300s, in Prague and most of the Bohemian empire, the Catholic Church was booming. Times were good. Profits gathered from indulgences kept meeting and beating expectations. Every young go-getter's dream was to hitch his wagon to the Catholic gravy train.

But Jan Has was an oddball. He had it in his head that the Church was cheating the people by collecting indulgences.

A rich noble kills his mother and kicks the family dog. Obviously, the 'Man Upstairs' does not approve of such behavior, so the rich noble slaps a few bills in a priest's palm, mumbles a Hail Mary, and ta-da—the sin is gone. During two-for-Tuesdays, you could sin twice for the price of one.

Hus didn't sit, stew, and complain to his bar buddies—he started a revolution. He believed that people did not need the Church to abolish their bad behavior. People could save themselves. Grab a Bible, look up to the sky, and make your wish—no church required. This is the same message Martin Luther, with the help of the printing press, made famous a hundred years later.

Not surprisingly, the Church did not react kindly to Hus's message and his band of rowdy brothers. They asked him to come for a pleasant sit-down and discuss the matter. He arrived for tea, but before the sugar dissolved, they burned him at the stake. This started the Hussite Wars, which lasted for over 20 years.

The result of the long war was nothing. Catholics won and the indulgence business was booming again. Not until Martin Luther stabbed his knife into the church door at Wittenberg did the would-be Protestants start up the fight again.

In 1526, the Hapsburg family took over the place. The Hapsburgs were a cultured and business-orientated family who brought science and commerce to the city. It was a prosperous time—Prague became the place to be. If you wanted to be a 'somebody', you had to be seen mingling in the high society of Prague. Astronomers, painters and poets went to hang out in Prague.

The good times lasted for one hundred years.

The hundred good years were quickly followed by a string of bad years. It was a reckoning for all that goodness. Of Prague's total population, 60 percent was lost in the Thirty Years War. A hellish fire erupted that destroyed most of Prague. And finally, with the citizens battered, bruised, and burnt, the Plague arrived and put 13,000 out of their misery.

The 20th Century—What a Nightmare That Was

At the beginning of the 20th century, things were looking pretty good for Prague. True, it was no longer the central hub of Europe—Vienna had that honor—but it did have a rich economy thanks to the Industrial Revolution.

The Austro-Hungarian Empire was not tyrannical. It held Prague on a long leash and left it free to move this way and that. Prague used the freedom to move up. It grew, expanded, and made its people prosperous and comfortable. A citizen in Prague in the year 1900 felt he had it all and the future could only get better.

World War I was not positive for a lot of people on the European continent. But it was good for the Czech people. Because Austria was on the team that lost, it was not allowed to keep its empire after the war. As a result, Czechoslovakia was born—a nice little country with Prague as its capital. The first president, Tomáš Masaryk, sat proudly in the Prague castle just like Charles IV did so many years before.

World War II was not positive for Czechoslovakia. The Czech people lost their country even before the war started. Hitler just walked down from Germany and took it, and nobody did anything about it. For the entire war Prague was draped with German tapestries.

A proud moment during the war was when a group of Czechs assassinated a powerful German,

Reinhard Heydrich. The drawback to this success was Hitler's retribution: he completely obliterated a Czech village from the face of the earth. All the villagers were shot and every building bulldozed—nothing remains but an empty field.

But finally after many trials, struggles, and horrors, World War II ended. German decorations were taken down and the Germans were forcefully asked to leave. Prague was the capital of Czechoslovakia once again.

The celebratory cold cuts were still fresh when the Russians decided that it was their turn to decorate the city. Prague's new color scheme was going to be red. The dark cloud of Communism loomed above as Prague became the stage to a puppet show that lasted for over 40 years. The once rich and beautiful city turned to a decaying and economically dead city. For citizens, it meant that putting fresh bread on the table depended on knowing the right people who could pull the right strings.

In 1989, when the USSR's grip loosened, the Czech people decided they had had enough of the misery. It started with a group of university students but ended with thousands of men, women, and children gathered at Wenceslas Square, demanding the Communists step down.

The Russians left and they took Communism with them. Prague castle became the seat of a democratically elected president of a free market economy.

The 21st Century

So far things are going relatively well.

Dessert: The Good King Wenceslas

Six hundred years ago, Wenceslas Square was a horse market. Today, the only horse you will see is the statue in the center of the street carrying the legendary good King Wenceslas.

When the times come that the Czech people are at their darkest period, when the enemy is about to strike the final blow, when they need help the most, the statue of good King Wenceslas and his horse will come to life.

Bruncvik and The Magic Sword

A long, long time ago in Prague, there lived a young man named Bruncvik. He was at the age that requires adventure, a need to travel new lands and to prove his worth. A young maiden, Neomenia, who loved him very much, begged him not to leave. But he had to go —his blood was too hot to stay. He promised her he would return within seven years and marry her. With a final look into her tear-filled eyes, Bruncvik turned and set off to see the world. Prague was at his back; ahead lay the unknown.

And adventures he had. At sea, his boat was overtaken by a fierce storm. The boat and its crew were tossed onto the dreaded Amber Island, a place from which no one had ever returned. Two long and agonizing years passed with no hope of escape. All the men from the boat except Bruncvik died on the island. Their loss of hope drained all life out of them. Only Bruncvik had a reason to continue to live—his beloved future wife kept his heart pumping.

On the island were left only Bruncvik and an old man marooned on the island decades before. Bruncvik begged the man to help him off the island. The old man, seeing passion in the young man's eyes, revealed a secret: Every year a large bird flies over the island looking for prey. Bruncvik covered himself in horse's skin and sat waiting atop the biggest hill on the island.

Sure enough, the large bird came, picked him up in her sharp claws, and took him off the island.

Bruncvik was dropped in a nest amongst three baby birds. The hungry birds began eating away at the horse's skin. Bruncvik, free of the disguise, pulled out his sword, killed the baby birds, and jumped out of the nest.

He walked the lands until he came across a large lion fighting a multi-headed monster. Seeing that the lion was losing and tired, Bruncvik joined in the fight. After many days of fighting together with the lion, the monster was defeated. The lion and Bruncvik quickly became friends—fighting friends. They traveled the lands fighting monsters together.

During one strange adventure, where the queen of the lands tried to force Bruncvik to marry her, not only did he manage to avoid marriage, but he also managed to steal a magic sword. The sword had the special power of chopping off heads with a simple verbal command: "Blade, heads off". This magic sword made Bruncvik a great warrior.

After many years of rolling the heads of his enemies, Bruncvik's blood began to cool. He wanted to return to his love and future wife. He headed home with his loyal lion.

His adventures did not end upon his return. He discovered that Neomenia, who had waited for more than seven years, was to be married the next day. She could not wait for her true love any longer. But when she discovered that he had returned, she quickly called off the wedding and pledged her soul to the returning hero. Jealousy and rage took over the rejected husband-to-be. He rounded up his friends and plotted to kill Bruncvik. They surrounded him and attacked. But Bruncvik was a master fighter, and with his magic sword he separated them all from their heads.

Like all good legends, Bruncvik and the lovely Neomenia married and lived a long and happy life together, their pet lion always at their side.

The magic sword is hidden somewhere amongst the stones of Charles Bridge where it waits to this very day until it is needed again. Only one man knows the true hiding spot—King Wenceslas.

A day will come when Prague will be in its darkest hour. When all seems lost. When the enemy will be hours from defeating the Czech people. When that day comes, the Czech people will gather at the statue of Saint Wenceslas.

The stone of the statue will burn away, and from the ashes will emerge King Wenceslas. Sitting strong and firm on his horse, he will comfort the Czech people with his cry, "Sleeping Army of Blaník, rise from your slumber!" Thunderous noise will be heard as the long-sleeping army will rise from the mountain and heads towards Prague—towards their good master.

King Wenceslas will gallop to Charles Bridge and knock over a secret stone, revealing the location of the magic sword. Sword in hand and a bloodthirsty army at his command, Wenceslas will defeat the enemy. The motherland and its people will be saved from evil and returned to peace and prosperity.

Over a Couple Beers: What To Ask A Czech

Nobody can accuse you of ignorance for knowing next to nothing about the Czech Republic and its history. Countries like US, China, Russia, Italy, Greece, Britain all get honourable mention at some point in school and constantly appear in the news as they push and pull in world geopolitics. So without effort, via osmosis, these countries keep filling and updating our mental entries. Not so with the silent Czech Republic - that entry stays empty.

A small country which has existed only since 1993, it sits amongst all the other little countries in eastern Europe: Slovakia, Hungary, Moldova, Serbia, Ukraine etc. Unless you have a map of Eastern Europe over your bed it is easy to get all these little countries confused. And unlike Serbia, Croatia and Ukraine which have made infamous appearances on the world stage, the Czech Republic lives mouselike.

But history did not have to be that way. Czech history could of been a lot more violent. Plenty has happened in the last hundred years that had it gone less peacefully Czech would of made its public appearance. Czechoslovakia was quietly created in 1918 after almost 500 years under the umbrella of the Austro-Hungary empire. Then without much fanfare, because the Czechoslovakians were forced to surrender without fighting, Hitler strolled over and occupied the country. Then the Russia's marched in for their turn of occupation - again there was little resistance. Not until 1989 did the people invoke a peaceful uprising which resulted in sovereignty. A few years later with a handshake Czechoslovakia split into two separate countries - Czech Republic and Slovakia. The word that keeping appearing to describe these normally riotous events is peacefully. Czechs and Slovaks are aware and proud of their meekness and patience. It is because of their peaceful nature that you don't know anything about them.

I hope I have sufficiently convinced you that Czechs are a peaceful people. You should not hesitant to engage them. They will not be offended, they have collectively been through worse than a stranger asking them a few questions over dinner.

The best way to find out about Czechs and their history is to talk to one. A conversation will not only tell you what happened but how the people feel about it - how it impacted their lives. But what to talk about, what to ask? You could ask questions of the 'important historical dates' kind. But why waste your conversation on facts you can find out on wikipedia. Get into their heads ask about what they care about.

Questions To Ask

Here is a list of questions to ask. These questions are recent and ongoing issues that every Czech citizen has a strong opinion about. Ask these questions and you will not only get a history lesson but a glimpse into the Czech soul.

Question 1: Since the creation of Czechoslovakia in 1918 the two ethnicities of Czechs and Slovakians have been coexisting within the borders of one country. Then in 1993 Czechoslovakia was split into the separate countries of Czech Republic and Slovakia. Why did Czechoslovakia split? *Has life improved for both the Czechs and Slovaks since the split? Was it better together?*

Question 2: At least 200,000 Roma's, commonly know as Gypsies, live in the Czech Republic. The Roma's are considered to be asocial and relations between the Czech's and Roma's are terrible. Most Czechs consider them a burden on society and claim they do nothing but steal, take advantage of generous social programs, live in squaller and destroy everything around them. The Roma's on the other hand feel they are a persecuted minority. *What should be done about the animosity between the Czech's and Romas?*

Question 3: Right after the ousting of the communists in 1989 the capitalists arrived and started buying up public assets. Everything owned by the communists was up for sale - the utility companies, buildings, land and natural resources rights. Although an effort was made to make the sale fair with equal opportunities for all, it is almost unanimously believed that the process was corrupt and the politicians sold off the public assets for cheap to enrich themselves and their friends. To this day politicians are viewed as greasy palmed and corrupt. *How was the transition from communist ownership to private ownership accomplished? Was it fair?*

Question 4: Czech people are capitalists at heart. Since the forced implementation of communism after the second world war most Czech people were eagerly waiting for return of capitalism. There was great celebration when that day came in 1989 and everybody agreed it was a good thing. But surprisingly, now almost thirty years later there are some people looking back at the communist times as the good old days. Things were less hectic and life was generally easier they argue. The communist party has been slowly regaining ground and its political influence is once again on the rise. *Is life better under capitalism? What was better under communism? How is it possible, after all those years of struggle to get rid of it and the suffering it caused, that communism is slowly creeping back?*

Question 5: Czech joined the European Union in 2004 but it remains one of the few countries to not adopt the Euro. The Czech President at the time, an economist, was determined to keep Czech out of the Euro. He claimed that the Euro would take too much fiscal control out of the hands of the Czech people and place it into the muddled bureaucratic machinery of the EU. At the time he was opposed by most Czechs because they felt the right thing to do would be to adopt the Euro. But given the last couple years of the Euro performance and problems with Greece, Czech are starting to see the wisdom of keeping their own currency. *Is Czech better off for keeping its own currency? Is the EU beneficial for the Czech Republic?*

Question 6: The Czech past was a religious one. Ancient churches are everywhere. Cities have cathedrals and small towns have chapels with holy ground cemeteries. Agricultural fields are protected with a statue of crucified Jesus. The large monument at the center of Old Town Square in Prague is of Jan Huss, the martyr who was burned for expressing his strong religious beliefs. Religion was once on the minds of all, but today Czechs are in the third spot as the most atheist group in the world behind China and Japan. Of course, the communism government did not encourage religion and let most of the churches rot but most people were not communists so it does not explain the current atheism. *Why is there such a disproportionally high percent of atheists in Czech compared to other countries in the region?*

Question 7: Looking at the last hundred years it is clear that Czech people are meek and have strong ethnic ties to their shared heritage and culture. Occupied and controlled first from the Austro-Hungarians, then Germans, then Russians, they regardless persist as a solid ethnic group. It is like none of it happened and they continue doing what they do. *How do Czech people explain the perseverence of their ethnicity?*

Hope to See You Around

I live in Prague and I feel comfortable in Prague. I can walk down any street and into any restaurant. For me all the little quirks and oddities of the culture are natural, I don't even think about it. The waiter is bringing me beer without asking – that is normal.

Last year I visited Istanbul. It was a culture shock for me. I did not know how to act, what the norms are, or even how to say hello. Whenever I arrived at a quit street I was to scared to go down it. I noticed local restaurants but did not go inside because I did not want to risk breaking some unknown social rule. Can foreigners eat here, do I need to take my shows off, should I say hello, can I sit anywhere I want? I had no idea. And that was still before even sitting down. I did not want to make a fool out of myself so I stayed away. I was clueless to everything so I did nothing. I limited my visit to tourist spots because I was afraid of making a major faux pas in front of the locals.

I missed out on experiencing the real Istanbul and had to stick to the tourists spots because nobody gave me a brief cultural rundown of how things work. That is why I wrote this book - I don't want what happened to me to happen to you. Prague has kind people and good food - there is no reason to hide from the locals. You should now know enough of Czech culture and norms to walk down a side street and walk into a local restaurant.

If you see me and there is an spot at my table, point to the empty seat and ask 'volno?' (is it free?). I will smile and nod. Sit down, order yourself dumplings with meat sauce and tell me how much you loved this book. The first Pilsner is on me.

Roman Jelinek
roman@pragueczechtravel.com
Prague – 2016

This Will Help You Blend

They speak a different language in Prague - Czech. Google Translate can help you learn the survival words. http://translate.google.com

Here is a list of the absolute minimum you need:
   Hello or goodbye: Ahoj
   Yes: Ano
   No: Ne
   Water: Voda
   Beer: Pivo
   Thank you: Děkují
   Please: Prosím

There are many ways to get around thanks to public transit. Here is the website locals use to find out what trains to take and when they leave. http://jizdnirady.idnes.cz/vlakyautobusy/spojeni/

If you need a map wait till you get to Prague and visit one of the many book stores. They have plenty of local maps to choose from.

If you need a practical tourist travel book to orientate yourself I recommend Rick Steves' Prague and the Czech Republic. I tell you that Prague is safe, but he tells you were the hospitals are.

If you need to go to a western type mall to buy Czech underwear and socks you can go to Palladium or Cerny Most.

Printed in Great Britain
by Amazon

My Song Matters

A book of Poems by Mary Bain

Introduction

My husband, Bob, is always very enthusiastic when he knows I have written another poem. He likes to hear me read it aloud and invariably asks me to repeat it several times!

I also like to hear poetry read aloud or performed. I have performed some of the poems in this book in a Christmas service or Sunday meeting. However, the majority were written as part of an ongoing conversation in my relationship with Jesus and Daddy God.

Usually these poems have flowed from my pen very easily, and have helped me to express some of my deepest emotions. 'The Journey' part of the book sets out chronologically this story of my life with Jesus.

I have been tremendously encouraged in my writing by both my husband and my family. Esther deserves a particular mention as, about two years ago she got me writing again by simply saying, "Why don't you just set a time, say 15 minutes and write down all your thoughts without pausing too much". I did so- and it was totally freeing!

"My Song Matters", (the title of the book and one of the poems) was written at a continuous worship event called David's Tent in 2013. It was in this atmosphere of creativity and freedom that God spoke to me about the importance of my poetry, because it is part of who I am, and it matters that I express it, rather than hiding it away!

I hope you enjoy the poems- the fun ones and the more serious ones, but mostly I hope they encourage you to also express the song that God has placed inside you!

Dear Niyi n Oyin,

God bless you & your lovely family! I hope this book is an encouragement to you – You have both been an inspiration to me! With much love,

Mary xx

Copyright © 2015 by Mary Bain

All rights reserved.

This book or any portion thereof may not be reproduced or used in any manner whatsoever without the express written permission of the publisher except for the use of brief quotations in a book review or scholarly journal.
ISBN 978-1-326-50095-5

London, United Kingdom

Mary Bain

e mail:marybain1@hotmail.co.uk

CONTENTS

Christmas

    6   The Donkey's Story
    8   The Stable
   12   Following You

The Journey

   14   Use my life
   16   One Life
   18   Acrostic Psalm
   20   Thank you
   22   New Day
   24   Use me
   26   Deep calls to Deep
   28   Your little Flower
   30   Sorry Prayer
   31   With Jesus a conversation
   33   You are here
   35   Heart Surgery
   37   All for Jesus
   39   Keep pulling my Heartstrings
   41   Speaking to Myself!
   43   Holocaust Tower
   48   Hidden Treasure
   50   God's love in Jesus
   52   River of Love
   55   Not Remote

56	Nothing without You
58	My Song Matters
60	Harvest Time
62	Here I am
64	Who are you listening to?
67	Who is my Neighbour?
68	Desire
70	Go Deeper
73	A Place to belong
75	My Redeemer
77	Faith has a Voice
80	There is Freedom!
82	Face to Face
84	Together with You
87	Burnt Ground
88	Abide in Me
89	Abba
90	Peace after the Storm

Easter

91	What have you done?
93	How many times?
95	How long, O Lord?

Family

98	Bain Babies
100	Wonderful Husband
101	Dear Bob- 25 years
103	To Ma – a Lily
105	My Daddy and the Wedding

CHRISTMAS
The Donkey's Story

I was surprised at her weight
I'd carried her before
The sweet, gentle girl
My master had chosen for his bride
But this time it felt different.

The journey was long, so long, uneven underfoot
And all the time I could feel her pain-
Irregular at first, then stronger, more urgent
It crashed through my body from hers
And at last I realised why.

She gave birth in Bethlehem
For that was our journey's end
And my back became her pillow
My breath warmed the air
Of that dirt-filled stable

Where she brought forth her little son.

Now, if you've ever felt foolish
Nothing special and quite dumb
Know that they said the same of me-
But it's not true- you can lift up your head!
For if I, like Mary, was chosen
Then there's hope, real hope, for you too
And for everyone!

Mary Bain December 2010

The Stable

I've got used to being like this,
The cold and silent darkness
Untrodden floor and smelly straw.
No one comes near me now.
There was a time
I can just remember
When it was different.
There was life and noise
Hens clucking, cows munching,
And, at least once a day,
A man who swept me clean
Leaving fresh hay
Pleasant sweet smelling days! *–sigh–*
Gradually things changed
Many years went by
I suppose other places were found to house
The inn-keepers animals
And I, left unfit, unkempt, neglected
Slowly falling into decay.

I had got used to it

Resigned myself

Resenting only the ever-present rats

Whose gnawing disturbed my solitude.

-Pause-

But what is this?

The light, so bright, so painful,

Voices...

People coming inside!

A donkey with them

Tired from a journey

I catch a glimpse of my old friend-

The inn keeper,

But the other two?

Strangers- a man, a lady,

A quiet calm surrounds them

-slow-

New fresh hay is laid on my floor

A sense of expectancy arises within me

-quicker

How can this be?

I feel special, important even,
I wait.
-pause-
Warmth pervades my whole being
The lady is lying in the straw
Her husband very close
Attending to her.
The donkey is also near
His breath softly stroking her wavy hair
The whole earth seems to pause
-pause-
Her labour is long, not easy,
Painful, arduous,
After the exertion already of a long journey,
But she is surprisingly strong
I sense, supernaturally
Strengthened and supported
And so at last her cries of pain
Give way to tears of joy...
And she cuddles closely her new-born child.
Immediately I feel His love

It emanates from His small shining face

Piercing the dark and smelly corners of my being

If only I had known

How to make Him welcome!

I could have got myself ready...

-pause-

But no, it's ok

His love is so strong

He understands everything!

No room for regret.

<u>He chose the place</u>

<u>This stable for His own!</u>

The joy is indescribable!

I will never be the same again,

Since the day I met Jesus my Saviour!

    Mary Bain   December 2003

Following You

The wise men followed a star
The shepherds followed the angel's directions
You call me to follow You.
How can we refuse such an invitation?
I can see you calling the fishermen
'Leave your nets, come follow Me'!
Your voice encourages,
Your eyes beckoning
Your arms welcoming-
I have a compelling desire to follow You.

But You don't promise an easy path
'Take up your cross daily', You said.
Daily, not just once.
'They will lead you where you do not want to go'.
You said that to Peter.
And then You said, 'Follow Me'.
You laid down Your life.

So I need to lay down mine.
You surrendered Your will
So I need to surrender mine.
You came to serve others
So I too must be a servant
The way to live is to follow You.

With my whole heart
My whole being
My whole life
Like the sheep follow the shepherd
I will follow You
And as the wise men gave their gifts
I will discover the joy
Of a life given to Jesus.

Mary Bain 24th Dec 2001

THE JOURNEY
Use my life

Lead me on my new road

I'll try not to look back

With my eyes on You, Jesus

Nothing shall I lack

Teach me to be humble

To love my fellowmen

Teach me to be like You Lord

How to talk to them.

How to love them with Your minute care

If only I could count every hair!

Lord please enter my unworthy home

Cleanse me to live for You

In the shadow of Your love

Ready to do Your will.

Use me, here I am

Unworthy and afraid

A weak vessel indeed
But Yours, completely saved.

I can do nothing on my own
I need the right attitude Lord!
Still I struggle and long for the peace
You alone can afford.
Show me the way, how to live,
Teach me Jesus-
I want to learn.

Mary Bain   April 1980

One Life

A pebble drops
The ripples spread wide
Reflecting, touching
Reaching even to the side.

A grain of wheat falls
Buried, it lies alone
But life is bursting upwards
Many seeds have grown!

A life given to You
Precious in God's eyes
What you do and what you say
Touches so many lives.

A heart open to receive
From His outpouring love
Dies to self, lives for others
Giving praise to God above

A cross, a grave, a life given
No hope except for Him
He made His life count, now our turn
Don't throw it away- give it to Him!

Mary Bain March 1999

Acrostic Psalm

All that I am I give to You

Be magnified in my life

Come and dwell within me

Deliver me from my own ways

Enter my heart Lord Jesus

Fill me up completely

Govern all my days

How I yearn for You

I want to be Yours and Yours alone

Jesus, I love You

King of my heart as well as the Universe!

Lord of power and might

Majesty, Your Majesty!

Now I kneel before You

O how I long to do Your will

Pleasing You is my desire

Quiet and at peace with myself

Resting, gently resting with You

Saviour, I thank You

Truly You have loved me

Unto You I offer my life

Visit me again and again

Wherever You go, I will follow

Expect me to stay by You

You are my life, my joy, my One and Only!

Zeal for Your presence consumes me!

Mary Bain October 1999

Thank you

Thank you for coming into my life
Thank you for changing me
Thank you for enabling me
Thank you for bringing hope
Thank you for giving blessings in abundance
Thank you that I can trust You
Thank you that I can depend on You
Thank you for being there
Thank you for being faithful
Thank you for life in all its fullness
Thank you for listening to me
Thank you for keeping and protecting me
Thank you for giving me a job to do,
a purpose for living,
Thank you for the joy of serving and giving
Thank you for the world You made
Thank you for relationships, for family,
Thank you for my husband, who tends me like a garden
Thank you for my children, who look to me for nurture

Thank you for giving me the capacity to love
and to give

Thank you for health in body and mind

Thank you for freedom to worship You

Thank you for my home and garden,
all that You have given

Thank you for food and clothing

Thank you for caring for the smallest detail

Thank you for being my Father and loving me,
Your child

Thank you that I belong to You

Thank you for Your Holy Spirit,
infilling and strengthening me

Thank you Jesus, my Master and my Lord.

Mary Bain January 2000

New Day

There's a new Beginning

Grace is awakening

Sufficient for every need.

Hope is rising

Faith is stirring

Strength which comes from You alone.

Joy breaks forth

Warming my heart

Comforting my mind

Pain fades away-

Laid upon You.

Thank you Jesus

You can take it and I can make it

But only in You!

Forgive me, and give me

Your grace, to let go.

It's not my place

To hold the stone.

I'm dropping it
For You.

The cross is so necessary
Without Your love,
Your death
I cannot survive.

But with You, I can make it.
Thank you that You can take it!
It's a New Day-
Help me to laugh with you!

Mary Bain August 2001
(forgiving someone at a Summer Camp)

Use me

I'm waiting

Actively waiting

In expectation

Of what You are going to do.

I'm offering

All of me offering

Use me as Your vessel

Your servant.

Flow through this channel

I will not resist

The high current of Your Love and Power.

Make it, break it, take it –

Actively seeking

Actively reaching

Giving

Yielding

Serving

Healing

Freeing

Releasing

Being Jesus – to the people!

Mary Bain March 2004

Deep calls to deep

How can I express

All I feel I want to say?

Your love is stirring, calling, drawing me,

Smouldering within.

I want people to understand

The life that You give,

The freedom there is

In knowing You.

As Paul says,

Everything else is rubbish

Nothing important –

There is no meaning

If You are not real.

If You are not lifted up

Glorified and praised.

If You are not the centre.

Touch me again!

Place Your hand on my soul

Burn it deep

I so want to serve You!
Only You,
Nothing else will do.
My whole being is reaching, desiring, stretching
For You.
There is so much joy,
So much peace,
I am complete, when found
By You!

Mary Bain November 2004

Your little Flower

I want to come through
Walking with You.
Each day, growing in trust
I really must
Keep my eyes on Your face,
No one else taking Your place.
I will let You come close
You care for me the most
Looking deep into my eyes
You understand all my sighs.
You believe in me
And You want me to be
Sitting at Your feet
Whole and complete
Your Mary, Your little flower
Open to receive
To learn and to believe
To be Your disciple
Knowing who I am.

I reach up and take Your hand,
You are helping me to stand.
Thank You!

Mary Bain September 2006

Sorry Prayer

Open my eyes

Fixed upon Your face

Looking intently

I'm in need of Your grace.

Open before You

The sorrow and pain

I feel all You have suffered

You call out my name.

I am sorry, so sorry

For how I have been

Please accept me, receive me

In all my shame.

Lift up my head

Exert Your claim

I am Yours

I am willing, I love You!

Please help me to change. Amen

Mary Bain September 2006

Talking with Jesus

Look up My child

Gaze upon My face,

I'm smiling at you!

Thank you, thank you Jesus

I love You so much

My heart is bursting with love for You!

Give Me your hand My sweet one.

You can trust Me completely

I am holding you.

My Lord, my Master, my Owner

I belong to You.

Pierce my ear, I want to stay with You forever.

Come forth beautiful daughter

Step out of the grave

I want to dance with you!

I long for You with all my being
Take me, take me nearer to You
I give You everything!

Come with Me, My child
Run through the pain and the sorrow
I understand completely,
I know you so well.

I'm coming, I'm coming My Lord!
Running into Life.
You are with me, and I need not fear
I am kept by the power of Your love.
With You, my yoke is easy, and my burden is light.

Mary Bain November 2007

You are here

It is so good to know

You are here

Your love, Your peace surrounds me

Sometimes I feel so insecure

Frightened and lost inside

Like a little girl again

Desperately clinging to her Mummy's skirt

Don't go Mummy, don't go!

Something has been lost,

Never to be recovered

Gone forever!

I need to remember that

You are here.

I am not alone

I can rest in Your arms

There is a deep stillness

Even in the midst of turmoil

Because of You, my Lord

Because of You.

I honour You,

Truly, You are all I need.

Mary Bain April 2008

Heart Surgery

Thrust in Your sickle
This harvest is ripe
Don't hold back from hurting me
I need that knife!

Take me, my heart
And cut out the mess
Get rid of the deceit
The pride and the bitterness.

Don't be over gentle
I need a ruthless scrape
I want to be a consecrated vessel
No way of escape.

I'm waiting, earnestly ready
Holding open my heart
Through the pain, I'm keeping steady
I'm ready to be taken apart

Please, please make me holy

I am desperate for Your touch

I am longing for You only

I love You so, so much!

Mary Bain April 2008

All For Jesus

It's all from You
You meet my every need
All from You,
All, all from You
Nothing we can give,
Nothing we can do
It's all, all from You.

It's all, all about You
You are supreme, majestic, King and LORD
Who can come against You?
Who can argue with You?
You are Wisdom, Strength, Power and Might
It's all, all about You.

It's all, all for You
My Jesus, my LORD,
My Saviour, my Friend
What can I give? – You deserve everything.

You gave Your life, You lost it all
Nothing else will do
But to give my life in service to You
It's all, all for You.

I'm giving it all, all to You
All the pain, the bitterness, the loss
The sickening feelings in my stomach
My breaking heart
The deepest and darkest fears
The trembling and desperate emptiness
Here it is –
I'm handing it to You
I know You can take it
Because of the Cross.
Because You stretched out Your arms
And gathered me
In that painful embrace of Love
I'm giving it all, all to You.

Mary Bain April 2008

Keep pulling my heartstrings

I want to know You more,

Much more than I do.

I want to be so close to You

That it hurts

To feel Your love,

Your pain, Your rejection,

Your denial and betrayal.

Do I know what I am asking?

"Can you drink the cup that I drink?" You said.

I don't know if I can,

But I want You to keep pulling my heartstrings.

Holy Spirit, keep doing it!

Please keep me open, not bitter

Open to all You want to do

In me, and through me

Despite the pain

I want to say, "Your will be done,

Not mine, but Yours.
Help me to cry,
If that is needed
You knew how to weep
When you had lost a good friend
Help me, work a change in me
I am willing to be different.
I give You this too

My emotions, my pain, my inner being
You know me so much better
Than I even do myself!
Bring me into line
Into all You have for me to be
I am willing.
I am placing myself on Your altar
Accept this sacrifice,
And burn me up in the Fire
Of Your Love.

Mary Bain April 2008

Speaking to Myself!

Don't remove yourself from reality

Keep in touch

Express yourself

Say Hello, Good Morning!

Touch, hug, love

Keep things in perspective

Know the Truth:

God is real

Jesus loves me

I have His life in me

I am a new person

I have freedom

I have value

I have purpose.

Stay close

Allow Him access –

So you don't grow cold.

His love frees you

Frees others too

To be the person He has made you to be

Open and responsive

That is where I want to be!

Mary Bain May 2008

Holocaust Tower

(written in Berlin after visiting this museum)

They closed the door

A heavy door, guarded closely.

Dark grey slabs, cold to touch

Rose alarmingly high above me

Stretching up and up

And at the top

The light shone in.

But I could not reach it

There were steps, a ladder,

But out of grasp

And ending

Far short of the light.

Nevertheless,

The light seemed friendly

And warm.

Also from above came sounds

Children playing

Cars driving by
Even birds singing
So normal –
Freedom, falling down from above
Friendly, familiar freedom.

The contrast almost unbearable
With the cold desolate condition
Of myself.
Alone, so, so alone. Yet...
Not alone.
Pause
More and more are pushed inside
Scrabbling, clamouring crowds
Bodies pushing
Forcing me into a corner
Naked, cold bodies
Devoid of all human dignity
Deliberately devalued and debased
Degradation at its worst
Absolute total dog shit.

Down, down I went
Under this mass, squashing me,
Squeezing the life-breath out.

Then the sweet, sickly smell of gas
I started to fight
Looking upwards, I struggled
Climbing, pushing, reaching
All around
Others doing the same
Towards the light
The air
Freedom
One thought only –
To reach the light,
To escape this dark hole
This hell of insanity.

Frantically I fought
And as I fought
I thought I heard them laughing

Mocking my fate.

And then, He came
Or rather His voice
Speaking into my heart
My desperate, crying heart
"My child, come to Me
Here I am
I know your pain
I, too, have been here
You are so close, please come
Be My friend!"

I reach out my hand.
"Lord, here I am,
I'm sorry I am so late
In giving myself to You"
I feel His friendly welcome
"It's ok" He seems to say,
"Just forgive. My grace is all you need"
And there, in the abyss of man's abuse

I am released

I step forth

Into the real light

Shining into eternity

Friendly, familiar freedom

With Jesus.

Mary Bain June 2008

Hidden Treasure

Cleaning, polishing and restoring
God sees the hidden treasure in us
Others may only see rubbish
But He is the antique guy-
He sees what is hidden.

When the enemy tells you, "You're worthless!"
God looks inside you and sees hidden treasure
When you put Him on the throne of your life
He'll help you to overcome your past
Resist temptation
Breakthrough your self-imposed limitations
And start accepting that
In His eyes you have <u>great worth.</u>

<u>The divine nature is in me!</u>
I am someone who is being <u>transformed</u>
<u>Into His likeness.</u>
I am an item that just needs to be cleaned

Polished and restored

In order to become valuable again.

Mary Bain July 2008

God's Love in Jesus

Your love

Smiling kindly, tenderly

Reaching into my heart

Gently, carefully unfolding my clutching fingers

Freeing and setting me free

Enquiring, concerned even with the smallest detail

Listening and laughing

Helping me to laugh.

How amazing, surprising and liberating

You really love me!

There's no pretending

No ulterior motive

No demanding

Just warmth and affection

Held and hugged

Close and safe

For a long time...

And then challenged to step forward

With that love still burning

Still freeing

Still working

But this time, for others as well

For others to see, and feel, and experience

And also <u>to be changed</u>

In the same way as I am!

Mary Bain September 2008

River of Love

You won't love me any <u>more</u>

If I do good, help people, be nice

You won't love me any <u>less</u>

If I'm selfish, self-centred, nasty, uncaring

You just love me <u>completely, fully</u>

<u>For who I am</u> –

A unique expression of Your creativity

Through my mother's conception

The human and the divine

Coming together

To make me, Mary.

You love me

You know all about me

You are totally familiar with my thoughts and desires

As well as what has happened to me

Each day of my life.

And You love me –

Not diminishing, not increasing

But pounding away

Constant, fervent, passionate love for me

Unchanging –

Reaching into the very depths of my being

Urging me to respond.

Yes, I love it

When I see Your love shining out

In someone's face,

Someone's eyes, or

Their kindness- in words,

A hug, a kiss, a helpful act.

It's so beautiful

Your love expressed

So warm and inviting

So freeing and forgiving

So full of joy and laughter

Carefree and funny-

Light and liberating

I want to flow in that River
Totally caught up with You
Enjoying Your love
As I continually love others
Show me Father!
Keep showing me!

Mary Bain January 2009

Not Remote

How can we ever think of You as remote?

You came and lived among us-

You rubbed shoulders with us

You understand what it feels like

To be human.

So good to realise this

You came, You lived, You died,

You wore the T shirt!

You know everything about how it feels

And so You can help us through life

In all its complexities

In fact- You were victorious

A winner in it all-

And because of Your victory

We can also be victorious in life

Step by step

As we walk in Your shoes.

Mary Bain February 2009   (written on a London underground train)

Nothing without You

Will never be able to do anything

Outside of Your love

Relationship with You

The bottom line of everything I do.

You love me for who I am

Not what I do

Don't slip back into religion

Trying to be good, faking it

Touch me Jesus

Take control

Step into the Driver's seat

I only want to be close

To You.

You take Your place-

Above everything

And everyone else.

Then my life will make sense

And I can be
All You have called me to be
I am waiting on You!
Here is my heart
Here is my heart
Here is my heart
You can have it all.

Fill me completely
No room for anything else
Flooded out with You
Desperate for You
I rest in Your approval
Don't need to do anymore
Don't need to be anyone else
Just as I am
I come to You.

Mary Bain March 2009

My Song Matters

My song matters
I have a song and I need to sing it.
My song makes a difference in the world
To those around me.
You are making me, and shaping me, and forming me-
So I can sing the song of Mary; (insert your own name!)
The song of my life with You.

Telling all that You have done
And all that you are doing-
A beautiful melody
With some painful notes
But many sweet moments...
A song of victory over sin,
Overcoming evil,
And pushing through in joy!
A triumph,
Unglimpsed by many,
But totally appreciated by You

And a few.....

Who know me better!

Help me to sing the song,

Expressing all the joy

You have put in me.

All the investment

Is appreciated.....

I know that I am loved by You.

Mary Bain   1st September 2013

Harvest Time

Remember Harvest Festivals in church,
Giving thanks for God's goodness
The crops all safely gathered in!
Colourful, exciting-
We brought along jam
Ma had made from raspberries,
Big fat marrows grown by my Dad,
Large brown eggs, laid by our chickens;
All sorts of tins from the cupboard too!
A great celebration and a time to give,
To share with others in need.

Jesus talked about a harvest time
"Not four months away," He said.
"But the time is now.
The fields are white- ready for harvest."
It's harvest time! And we are the fruits in the jam,
We are the vegetables- carrots, potatoes, marrows
All shapes and sizes!

We are even the eggs, perfectly formed
Carrying a promise of new life;
Or the tins, shiny and modern,
Full of good things!

All different, all special
We all need to be safely gathered in.
We are the harvest-
Look around, here we are!
Are we ready to be gathered home?
There is such a celebration in heaven
When even one sinner comes home!
Give Jesus your heart, every part.
When you give your heart,
Like ripe apples ready to drop,
The rest of you follows!

Let's be part of heaven's Celebration
Giving ourselves, bringing others too.
It's Harvest time!
Rejoice, you are coming Home! Mary Bain September 2013

Here I am

Here I stand
Before Your throne
With no righteousness of my own
Naked, transparent
And completely known by You.

Here I will stay
In awe of Your majesty
Covered by Your grace
Clothed in fine linen, redeemed
By the blood of the Lamb.

Here I kneel
Overwhelmed by Your beauty
Undone through Your love
I feel Your touch
The thrill of knowing You.

Here I will wait

For all eternity, Your warmth in my heart

At rest in Your presence

Enveloped in Your love

Forever worshipping My LORD.

Mary Bain September 2013

A Choice

Who are you listening to?
Who told you that you were naked?
Who told you that you were unloved?
Who told you that I do not exist?
Who are you listening to?

You have a choice to whom you listen
I also have a voice, which you can hear
I am the Word of God
I am Living Breath
My sheep listen to My voice

Who are you listening to?
Whose voice do you believe?
Amid the clamour and confusion
Where can you find the truth?
Who are you listening to?

There is an enemy who wants to deceive you
He comes in many shapes and forms
It isn't easy to spot deception
When clothed in beauty, desire and pride
I am the Truth that you need

Who are you listening to?
What songs do you play?
Whose conversations impress you?
Whose voice whispers on the darkest day?
Who are you listening to?

Here I am, and I am waiting
Just one look, one word, all I need
I am the conversation you are missing
I am your Lover singing over you.
Quieten your heart and listen to me

Who are you listening to?
When can I spend time with you?
Where have you set your affection?

What can we work on together?
Who are you listening to?

I am here and always have been
My heart is open wide
I affirm you my chosen, precious one
You are my son, whom I love
In you, I am well-pleased.

Who are you listening to?
Who told you that you were naked?
Who told you that you were unloved?
Who told you that I do not exist?
Who are you listening to?
Quieten your heart and listen to me

Mary Bain September 2013

Who is my neighbour?

My neighbour is the one completely different to me
My neighbour is the one bleeding and dying
in the road
My neighbour is the one from whom I have
felt nothing but rejection and hatred
My neighbour is the one crying out for help
My neighbour is the one who is in desperate need
My neighbour is the one I cannot walk by and ignore
My neighbour is from a different culture to me
My neighbour is someone I find hard to understand
My neighbour is the one I usually avoid
Because he usually avoids me
My neighbour is my enemy. Who is my neighbour?

My neighbour is a Jew and I am a Samaritan.
Or is it? My neighbour is a white English guy
and I am a black Nigerian.
Who is _my_ neighbour?

Mary Bain   6th October 2013

Desire

Here I am

Waiting

In eager anticipation

And expectation

Of an encounter with You.

My Lover is coming

His breath

I can feel it!

The warmth surrounds me

Tangible...

Setting me free.

How I adore You!

When can I meet with You?

When can we touch

Cheek to cheek?

Breathing in Your peace.

I can feel You
All around me
Enjoying me.
There is a heat
Almost too much to bear
Except it tastes so sweet.

And You are bringing me forth
Like gold burnished bright.
I am consumed in the fire
And walk into the light...
Forever Yours.

Mary Bain   21st November 2013

Go Deeper

How can my heart express
The beauty of Your holiness?
All that is within me
Burns with Your holy fire.
My senses overflow
I am reeling, swimming over
I can't get enough
Of Your exquisite love.

You fill up my senses, Jesus
Abba, Father!
How much more? How much deeper?
There is no end to Your love.
No end to the joy of knowing You.

Please take me deeper
You can carry me.
I trust You to take me,
Take me with You!

I just want to live in Your presence.

More of You- now I understand;
Or begin to understand
The desire,
The pull of Your love
Your presence- who You are.

How can I express it?
Yet You ask me to do so.
I am yearning for more,
You pull me on,
Because love has to be expressed.
It is a giving love
Not for holding on to.
In the giving away, it gets stronger.

Love is for giving, not for keeping
I want to live in the giving
Of Your love;
And go deeper, dive further,

Till I am overwhelmed
Completely submerged, and totally drowned
In the Love that is You.

My wonderful, amazing Lover,
Saviour and Friend.
Comforter, Redeemer,
Daddy God!
My all in all,
My Master.
So amazed to belong to You!

Mary Bain   7th March 2014

A place to belong

I've found a place
I've found a home
You are my dwelling place.

I've found a place
Next to Your throne
A place where I belong.

I've found a place
Where I can be
Totally loved and totally free!

I've found a place,
My heart skips a beat
I can sit and listen at Your feet.

I've found a place
Where there is peace
When has sleep ever been so sweet?

I've found a place
I want others to know
The Father's heart, where they can go.

I've found a place
Where fear cannot be.
Come, find <u>your</u> place in God's family!

Mary Bain   8th March 2014

My Redeemer

You are my Redeemer

There is no one else

Not myself, not another

Who can save me from destruction

It is You and You alone.

No other Saviour, no other LORD

You stand alone.

And I am so glad

That You came for me

You are my One and Only

Redeemer and Lover of my soul!

It all belongs to You

The Universe, and everything in it.

Your hands shaped the stars

The earth, and every living creature

It was Your breath

That spoke them into being!

And You called me forth
Your child, from my conception
Your finger touching under my chin
Your gaze lovingly holding me
My Redeemer and my LORD!

Now I know my Redeemer lives
You have come and made Your home in me.
Where You are, I will be
There is nowhere else, no one else
No other place for me.

You are all that I need
Your love burning in me
Fill my soul with Your desire!
Each day I come, trusting
Lay my head upon Your shoulder
My Redeemer, and my Friend.

Mary Bain   17th November 2014
(*Acts 4:12 "There is no other Name given under Heaven by which men can be saved"*)

Faith has a Voice

He could hear,

No, he could actually feel the arrival of Jesus.

The hairs on his neck were standing on end!

Why was he so desperate?

So loud?- He could not stop crying out!

Had he missed Him before?

He was determined not to miss Him this time;

Whatever it cost- his dignity,

Annoying the people, breaking the rules-

Like the woman he'd heard about

The one with the flow of blood.

She had pushed through the crowd.

Blow the rules!

She had to get close to Jesus, to receive her miracle.

Faith has a voice.

Bartimaeus had to be heard!

He had to be noticed by Jesus.

He knew that this was his moment;

And everything hung on him being heard-
His voice reaching Jesus' ears...
As soon as he began to cry out, and kept on and on-
It was a done deal
There really was no doubt that the scales
would drop from his eyes
No doubt whatsoever!
Faith can move a mountain.
This- a small thing in comparison!
And God's heart is tuned in to the voice of faith.
It is the language of Heaven!
Faith has a voice

He heard Jesus stop,
Instructing one of them to call him.
Even before they spoke, he was getting up;
The beggar's cloak thrown to the ground.
No need for that anymore!
Eagerly he stumbled forward to the spot
where he knew Jesus waited.
Trembling all over, as if in a dream,

He heard the Master-

'What do you want me to do for you?

His heart felt as if it would burst with joy.

If only he could see the One his heart desired!

'My sight, Master. Please, I want to see!'

Faith has a voice

'Come on!' he heard Jesus encourage him.

'Your faith has made you well!'

And immediately the colours cascaded together-

A kaleidoscope of rainbow sensations,

Like the crescendo of a symphony.

He reeled in wonder,

At the beauty of the scene before him,

and the One who loved him

Laughing with pleasure at his healing!

With a light step and a firm resolve,

A rich man followed Jesus down the road.

Mary Bain   2nd February 2015

There is Freedom!

The bells are ringing out

The bells are ringing out

They're ringing out for FREEDOM.

Freedom! Freedom!

Freedom from restrictions

Freedom from the past

Freedom to be...

all you were created to be.

Inside your heart is a bell

A different bell for each heart

Unique and special

Crafted by the Master

Each one ringing and bringing

A unique sound.

Pomegranates and bells

Around the hem of the High priest's garment

as he served in the Holy place.

Keep the bells ringing!
If the bells are ringing, all is well!
Open hearts like pomegranates
With the bell in the centre
Right in the middle of your heart.

When the bells are ringing
It is FREEDOM.
Each one a different note
Together making a sound
The sound of Freedom.

Freedom reigns in this place
Showers of mercy and grace
Falling on every face
There is Freedom!
Freedom to be.....
Who you were called to be!

Mary Bain April 2015
"Now the Lord is the Spirit; and where the Spirit of the Lord is, there is freedom" 2Cor 3:17

Face to Face

My face tells a story

And the story is not finished yet.

We will behold You

Face to face.

Moses longed to see Your face.

Our faces express who we are.

Looking into one another's faces

Is not always easy.

We want to hide.

But You see us as we are,

And You love us.

Here I am,

Behold, see me-

The handmaid of the LORD;

Be it done unto me

According to Your word.

I can relax

And be

Who You called me to be.

You see me

You know me

And You love me.

You show me who I am.

You speak a name over me

Like Adam, of one mind with You

Called the animals the names

You wanted them to be called!

Your signature is written on me,

I belong to You

You bought me and You own me!

And You say to each one of us

"Never forget you are special.

Totally unique,

Totally loved,

Totally special!"

Mary Bain 5th May 2015

Together with You

My eyes are fixed on Your face

Your beautiful face

All around me has faded into obscurity

You are the focus of my life

You have my total attention

I wait on You

It is a joy to smile and feel Your touch

A joy to know Your affection

I have given You access

To everything in me

It all belongs to You

And I know the serious joy

Of being completely Yours

It is serious,

Because Your cross has marked my life

But it is also an amazing joy

And Freedom-to be given

Yielded to You
Complete, and yet expectant
Of all that is coming
Of all that we have to do, together!

There is nothing
There is no one
There is nowhere
I would rather be
Than with You
You in me, me in You
Your presence is everything!

Can we run together?
Can we scale the heights? Climb the mountain?
Or, can we walk through the valley
Calling to others
Responding to their cries
Loving and healing the broken,
The desperate and the dying?
Keep touching my heart

It is only Your love in me
That can shape the change that is needed
Truly You are the potter
I, the clay!
I yield my life to You.

And You speak to me about responsibility
I am willing to step up
Fear no longer has a place in me
This girl is growing up
At last.
Responsibility involves responding to You
Listening to Your voice
And stepping out
In faith
It is a Partnership
I am not alone, I can do this!
Together- with You.

Mary Bain 30th May 2015

Burnt Ground

My heart is fertile ground

Prepared ground

Ready to receive a seed

To grow and

Be fruitful and multiply.

Here I am

Burnt ground

I see and receive the vision-

A fruitful tree.

I am ready

Fertile ground

Burnt on the inside

Ready to receive

Clean and clear

For Your seed My Maker

And My LORD.

Mary Bain 14th July 2015

Abide in Me

Resting in Jesus

At home in Him

His presence in me

Surrounding me

Your favour surrounds us like a shield

I am Yours

The handmaid of the LORD

Carrying Your presence

At peace

Held in Your arms

Close to Your heartbeat

At One with You

I am safe

Kept in Your love

And Your glory is shining all around

Here I am

Abiding in You

And You

Abide in me.　　　　Mary Bain 18th August 2015

Abba

Daddy, my security is with You

This is where I belong

I have a place

I can snuggle under Your jumper

Feel Your warmth

Skin to skin

Touching Your love

Breathing Life into me

My Daddy!

It's all going to be ok

My Daddy is here

Loving me.

Mary Bain 24th September 2015

(thinking about little grandson Edward, under Daddy, Jonathan's jumper, helping him to warm up after being born)

Peace after the Storm

It's coming!

Keep your hand on the plough

Hold on

Steady.

Truth will prevail

Clear and straight.

Patience will have her perfect work.

Stand firm

In His Presence

In the transition place

Until everyone has crossed over.

We are together in this.

Mary Bain 3rd October 2015

EASTER

What have you done?

What have you done? What have you done?
You have crucified My son.
What have you done? What have you done?
The horror and the pain
The abuse, the guilt, the shame.
What have you done? What have you done?
You have crucified My son.

Can you explain? Can you explain?
How Jesus took the blame.
Can you explain? Can you explain?
The blood that covers you,
The truth that sets you free.
Can you explain? Can you explain?
How Jesus took the blame.

Will you come? Will you come?
You who crucified My son.
Will you come? Will you come?
There is forgiveness deep and wide
Healing flowing from His side
Will you come? Will you come?
You who crucified My son.
Will you come? Will you come?
I want to know <u>you</u> as My son.

Mary Bain May 2007

How Many Times?

Again and again and again

They flogged You

Again and again and again

The whip came down

Tearing Your flesh

With sickening persistence

Again and again and again.

And by Your stripes we were healed.

How many times Lord?

How many times must I forgive?

How many times Lord,

Do I have to forgive my brother?

Again and again and again.

And the wounds were opened

And the flesh was bleeding

Again and again and again.

No, not seven times
But seventy times seven –
How many times?
Many, many times
Forgive and forgive and forgive
Again and again and again.
The whip comes down
And the wounds reopen
And forgiveness flows
With the blood of Jesus.

Mary Bain September 2007

How Long O Lord?

They twisted the crown of thorns
Pushed it on Your head
And hit You again in the face.
How long O Lord?

How long O Lord
Must the abuse continue?
Cruel words spat out
Violence, derision and scorn
Defiling Your person.
How long O Lord?

Crucify Him! Crucify Him!
Take Him away!
The crowd are shouting
Panting for Your death
How long O Lord?

How long O Lord
Must You hang there in agony?
The nails tearing Your flesh
Your lungs bursting
Your heart breaking
And the mocking continues.
How long O Lord?

How long O Lord
Can the tears flow?
The women are watching
The pain unbearable
And still Your love reaches down to us.
How long O Lord?

How long O Lord?
Now it is finished, the battle over.
You were obedient to the Father's will
Even unto death
And all the world has seen

The Truth of Who You are
The Way back to the Father
And the Life freely given.

Mary Bain September 2007

FAMILY

Bain Babies

Joy awakening

New day dawning

Eager eyes and sunny smiles

Baby babblings

Bare feet patterings

Come to greet me

Precious surprise!

Closely cuddling

Small fingers touching

Trusting always

Eyes searching and bright

Quietly resting

Silently owning

My lap- it's theirs by rights!

Later more noisy

Hunger is shouting

Frolics in the froth

Of the bubbly bath!

Now dressed and ready

Breakfast is munching

But for me the early Bain baby is best!

Mary Bain Summer 1999

Wonderful Husband

Your love surrounds me

Like a blanket at night

I feel your arms

I smell your scent

Your warmth melting me.

I long for you

My heart is open, we come together

I am yours and you are mine.

I feel complete.

Mary Bain 2nd September 2003

Dear Bob – 25 Years

Like a brook, you are
Bubbling, energetic, brimming with life
Eager, enthusiastic, exciting to be with
With sparkling wit and shining eyes
    You sweep me along
In the budding of our love...

Like a well, I am
Wonderfully welcoming my lover
Waiting, listening and feeling at home
With familiar friendliness and tender arms
    You draw me up
In the unfurling of our love...

Like a stream, we are
Joined together in the sight of God
Blending and changing, and continually receiving,
With tender touch and a Father's love
    He makes us one

In the blooming of our love...

Like a rushing river, we are
Rapidly moving, learning to live, learning to love,
Our lives filled with fruitfulness
The noise of children's laughter echoes in our ears,
With a servant-heart and a constant love
   You share my life,
In the harvest of our love...

Still as a silent pool , we are
Reflecting and enjoying what God has done
Accepting and seeing, forgiving and freeing,
With arms of love and words of kindness,
We release each other,
in the perfect plan of God's love...

Mary Bain 7th July 2004

To Ma- a Lily

Opening up to receive

Receive my love

Gentleness

Soft petals unfurling

Freeing themselves

Receiving, receiving rain from Heaven

Drinking in the grace that comes from God alone...

And in the receiving-

There is a response,

From the heart

A Stirring

A Strong urgency

A Breaking through

From way down deep there rises

A Surge – now it comes-

Pouring, pouring forth

Like a never-ending waterfall

Sweet, smelling scent

Pouring out
Filling the whole room
Blessing, touching all who come
Your life is beautiful, Mother
A beautiful lily
Pure and lovely
Receiving and giving God's love.
Thank you.

Mary Bain 2006 (read at Ma's funeral Oct 2007)

My Daddy & the Wedding

I feel your hand holding mine
Work-worn, strong and firm
I am safe with my Daddy.
I know that you love me
Your grip is so tight
You don't want me to get hurt
As we cross the rainy street.

I see you in my mind's eye
Sad and alone at home,
The chores all done
The chickens fed
You didn't come to my wedding.

We asked your permission
But you were not sure-
We were young, no job and

Bob was not a Catholic...

You could not give your approval.
But we were in love.
We went ahead anyhow,
Not listening to your advice.

After years of blocking it out
My heavenly Dad has come to help.
I hold no bitterness, just regret
That we did not give you more respect
More time perhaps...to talk.

In my imagination
I have asked your forgiveness, Daddy
And I've seen your pain.

Father God helped me to picture you
Beside me, walking up the aisle.
"Who gives this woman?"
My Daddy answering,"I do."

And later holding my hand tightly
As we danced together (with Jesus)
At my wedding.

Mary Bain November 2013